D0426988

ALTOGETHER GIFT

ALTOGETHER GIFT

A Trinitarian Spirituality

Michael Downey

ORBIS BOOKS

Maryknoll, New York 10545

The Catholic Foreign Mission Society of America (Maryknoll) recruits and trains people for overseas missionary service. Through Orbis Books, Maryknoll aims to foster the international dialogue that is essential to mission. The books published, however, reflect the opinions of their authors and are not meant to represent the official position of the society.

To obtain more information about Maryknoll and Orbis Books, please visit our website at www.maryknoll.org.

Library of Congress Cataloging-in-Publication Data

Downey, Michael
    Altogether gift : a Trinitarian spirituality / Michael Downey
      p. cm.
    Includes bibliographical references (p.).
    ISBN 1-57075-333-4 (pbk.)
    1. Trinity. 2. Spiritual life—Catholic Church. I. Title.

BT111.2 .D69 2000
231'.044—dc21

                                    00-037473

British Library Cataloguing in publication data. A catalogue record for this book is available from the British Library.

Dominican Publications ISBN 1-871552-745

"The text is always written
under the sweet pressure of love."

Hélène Cixous

To God the Father, Love's Pure Light,
To Christ, revealed in earthly night,
To God the Paraclete we raise
Our equal and unceasing praise.

Quae stella sole pulchrior
Charles Coffin, 1736

Contents

Introduction

This book began as someone else's idea. In the spring of 1994, Catherine Mowry LaCugna, then Professor of Theology at the University of Notre Dame, was preparing conferences to be given to the Carmelite nuns at Quidenham in England. In the course of a telephone conversation about her upcoming trip, Professor LaCugna and I were discussing some of the ideas we had put together in our jointly written essay on "Trinitarian Spirituality" for *The New Dictionary of Catholic Spirituality*. "We ought to develop some of our ideas in a small monograph," she said. I responded with enthusiasm, not only at the prospect of developing a small book on a topic of great interest to me, but also because of the sheer delight I anticipated in collaborating with her further.

I did not know Catherine LaCugna all that well. We were simply colleagues who shared a commitment to doing a kind of theology rooted in Christian spiritual and mystical traditions. We did so in a spirit of friendship.

In June of 1994 over dinner at an Italian restaurant in Baltimore at the annual meeting of the Catholic Theological Society of America, Catherine and I made preliminary plans for a small book on Trinitarian spirituality. We agreed to meet again at Notre Dame in October of 1994 to begin work. But the illness that would eventually take her life at age 44 on May 3, 1997 prevented her from doing so.

Catherine LaCugna's death was, and is, lamented not only by her colleagues and students at Notre Dame, but by many of us in the Catholic theological community throughout the United States. Warmly appreciated by most readers, and sharply criticized by some theologians, LaCugna's *God for Us: The Trinity and Christian Life* did more, perhaps, to stimulate thinking and discussion about the doctrine of the Trinity in Roman Catholic circles in the United States than any theological work since Karl Rahner's *The Trinity*. Her work helped bring three insights of enduring value to the fore: (1) whatever is said of the mystery of God must begin by attending to the Incarnate Word, Jesus Christ, and to the presence and action of the Spirit of God in human life, history, the church, and the world; (2) the mystery of God is profoundly relational, and this relational mystery is expressed in the language of Father, Son, Spirit; (3) the doctrine of the Trinity is an eminently practical teaching, expressing not only who and how we understand God to be, but what we think human persons are called to be and become: created to glorify God by living in communion with God and one another through Christ in the Spirit. These insights have shaped my own efforts to articulate the contours of a Trinitarian spirituality, both in the following pages and elsewhere.

In October of 1995 while I was at Notre Dame to give a conference, Catherine and I met for lunch. The cancer was clearly taking its toll. But she continued to teach, to read, and to research. Her interests in the last years of her life turned to a theology of the Holy Spirit. She didn't seem to have much energy or enthusiasm for our project. Nonetheless, I promised her that I would carry it forward.

What follows is a somewhat different treatment of Trinitarian spirituality than the one Catherine LaCugna and I first planned, since my own thought has developed in the years since her illness and death. Whatever there may be of value in this little book, I am certain that it would have been considerably richer if it had been undertaken as the shared project it was originally intended to be.

This volume appears as the church celebrates the great Jubilee 2000, a fitting time for reflection on the Trinity, the central mystery of Christian faith and life. In the last decade and more, there has been a renaissance of interest in the doctrine of the Trinity and its far-reaching implications for every dimension of the Christian life, inclusive of the spiritual life. Contemporary studies converge on the relational character of the mystery. But there has not been much attention given to the way in which the grammar of the Trinity might speak to the deepest desire of the human heart, the region of wound and wisdom wherein we long for loving communion with God and others. Language about the Trinity remains notoriously dense and complex. All too often it obscures the beauty of the mystery of which it is meant to speak.

My purpose is to make available in somewhat more accessible language that great mystery which the grammar of the Trinity seeks to express. It is my hope that my own grammar will not obscure what is on offer, but will instead be an invitation to receive the gift and the life that flows with and from it.

The book is intended for all who recognize the need for theological foundations in living the Christian spiritual life.

Some theological formation, however modest, will be of great help. At the same time this book is intended for spiritual seekers with no formal theological education, since its aim is to connect more technical treatises with personal life. But this is not a recipe book. It does not give directions or provide how-to steps and stages devised to manage or improve one's life. Rather, it holds out a vision and offers an invitation to receive the gift and take up the task of deification through which we participate in the very life of God. Thus, it may also be of some help to preachers who are called upon to relate the central mystery of Christian life to the practical demands of living the gospel in an increasingly complex world.

A Christian spirituality which is Trinitarian through and through is shaped by "gift" and "gift/ing," for the doctrine of the Trinity is a grammar by which Christians try to speak of the ineffable mystery of God's constant, eternal giving as gift. By accepting this gift we participate in the divine life. Our every response to this gift is a deepening in the dynamic of deification—being conformed to the person of Christ, brought into communion with God and others through the presence and power of the Holy Spirit.

This volume does not offer a comprehensive theology of the Trinity or a systematic presentation of Trinitarian spirituality. I have taken on a far more modest task. I simply draw attention to the gift given in the grammar of the Trinity so as to invite participation in the mystery of the three in one Love. Trinitarian spirituality is nothing more, or less, than living in and from this gift.

The title of this book is meant to convey three interrelated meanings. First, the love of God and the life flowing from it is altogether, that is, completely, gift. Second, this gift is the mystery of all three together in one Love. Third, by this gift we are invited, all of us together, into communion with the God whose name above all naming is Love.

For gifts received, a word of thanks:

To David Power, whose gift of language and language of gift continue to give life and light. In the course of our ongoing theological conversation I have been able to refine my thinking about the Trinity and to chart out the contours of the Trinitarian spirituality described in these pages.

To Jeremy Langford for his encouragement; to Mary Frohlich and to Robert Durback for their suggestions for improving the text; to Olga Medina and to John Cockayne for reading an early draft and offering encouraging words; to Eugene Lee, my student assistant at Saint John's Seminary, for his careful attention to the many details of this project.

To the Cistercian nuns of Santa Rita Abbey in Arizona, and to the Cistercian monks of Mepkin Abbey in South Carolina, for providing me with the opportunity to be embraced by the monastic rhythm of prayer and work within which this book was brought to completion.

To Robert Ellsberg, my editor at Orbis, whose abundant gifts overspill the editor's craft.

To Celine Allen, whose grace-filled hand has touched every page.

Finally, to the late Catherine Mowry LaCugna, who, even now, remains my colleague in God's grand economy.

Michael Edward Downey
9 January 2000
Baptism of the Lord

CHAPTER ONE

Learning to Speak of God:
Father, Son, Spirit

WE LEARN SOMETHING OF GOD in the process of naming. Names are connected to stories. And there are stories of naming. In some cultures, names are laden with meaning, as is the process of naming. Even though in most Western cultures the process of naming does not have the significance it once did, for many of us our names have a story, and there is a story to our naming. Our names do not pop out of a balloon. They are not spelled out in a vacuum. A name is given and received in relation to story. Whether the name is that of a parent or grandparent, an aunt or an uncle, or perhaps a month of the year or a jewel, the giving and receiving of a name—the process of naming—carries with it the hope that the bearer of the name will embody certain characteristics, virtues, qualities of the one whose name is borne. As the child hears the story of her grandmother, it is perhaps Grandmom's warm heart, generous table, and wide circle of family and friends that she is urged not to forget as the story is told and retold. It is, then, in the granddaughter's own living, the spelling out and telling of her own life's story,

17

that she continues Grandmom's story. Through her grand-daughter, Grandmom's legacy, her distinctive way of living, continues from one generation to the next. The story may be enriched. Sometimes the hopes at the heart of the process of naming go unfulfilled.

In Christian tradition, a child is sometimes named for a saint. It is the parents' hope not only that their child will embody the virtues of that saint, but that the child will participate in the blessed communion which the patron now enjoys. Within the Christian story, the child, in the company of the patron saint, is surrounded here and now by that cloud of witnesses who have gone before us. More to the point, in the process of naming within the Christian story, a child is always named in the name of the Trinity: Father, Son, Spirit.

Unlikely as it may seem, at the time of my birth there was no one in my family, near or distant, who bore the name "Michael." But, the story goes, it was my father's desire that I be named for Michael the Archangel, because Michael was the defender of good against evil, caught up yet undefeated in the battle between the darkness and the light. But there is more to the story of my being named. My father said that I was to be called "Michael," a name not his own, because he wanted me to have a life of my own, to find my own way, not bound to follow in his footsteps. He did not want me to live in his, or anyone else's, shadow.

Well named indeed! For I find myself daily caught in the struggle between darkness and light, overwhelmed from time to time by the magnitude of evil that can weigh so heavy on the human heart as it struggles inch by inch toward a glimmer of a distant light: by faith, in hope, through love. No archangel's wings on this Michael. And no dangling sword of silver or gold unsheathed in the face of the enemy. Rather, two clay feet hobbling along, stumbling in fits and starts as I make a way even when there seems to be no opening ahead, moving forward in the simple and sometimes shaky confidence that love and light will prevail over all evil and darkness. Well named, too, because I learned early on to trust my own lights, no matter how dim they may seem at times. I had to walk my own way, to follow my own path. There seemed no other way to go.

My father never expected me to do it his way. He gave me life, and gave it freely, as he gave me my own name, without one iota of expectation that I would grow up to be just like him or pay him back for all that he had given me. I never called him "Father." I called him "Dad." And as he grew sicker and sicker, and as he lay dying, I called him once again, "Daddy." Now that he is gone from us, and his story continues on in and through his only son, I recognize more clearly the gift that he was and is precisely as father.

Speaking of God: Old Testament

God is revealed in history in the names "Father," "Son," "Spirit." In recent decades, persuasive cases have been made for refraining from calling God "Father." The problem, however, is not with the name "Father." The problem lies in not hearing the story in which God is called "Father," in which the name "Father" is given, and in not explaining the name clearly enough. Retaining the names "Father," "Son," and "Spirit" as the normative way of speaking of God, even while recognizing the truth expressed in other ways of speaking of God, calls for a deeper understanding of the story to which these divine names are inextricably linked.

Naming God "Father" can be understood only in relation to story, to the many dreams and dreamers filling the pages of the scriptures, to the prophets and prophecies therein. The people of Israel called upon God, invoked the name of God, in diverse ways. Among the many ways in which they called upon God, they named God "Creator," "King," "Lord." God is in the heavens. God's is a voice that thunders. At other times God whispers. God is with the people in a pillar of cloud, a burning bush. God's hand saves, heart swells, womb quivers, eye watches. God leads and corrects, chides and guides. But, for the people of Israel, God's name is unspeakable, ineffable: YAHWEH—I am who I am; I will be who I will be. Yet this people yearns to call upon God, to respond to God's gift of life and love, to speak what cannot and, perhaps, should not be spoken: the name beyond all naming.

In the early stages of Israel's story, there is the recognition that God is active in history, present to creation. "It" is there, a force, something to be contended with, something quite real. A Someone? As the story unfolds, "It" or "He" is gradually recognized as One who addresses, who speaks, who makes an offer. This One calls forth, elicits a response, and makes a claim upon a people. In Israel's story, they are addressed, we are called, I am spoken to. Something is asked of them, of us, of me. Their response, our reply, my answer in the face of this One is "Thou," "You." "I" find that a claim is made upon me; I am called upon, addressed, named by a "Thou," a "You" whose name will ever elude me. And all of us.

In the Old Testament, God is named or addressed as "Father" roughly twenty times. The name has nothing to do with physical generation, but expresses God's deep involvement, relationship, with a people, with Israel. This is a people God has chosen and, even though they stray and err, God remains faithful to them because of love for them. The name "Father" conveys commitment and compassion; it bespeaks a loving protector who nourishes and sustains these people. Even when they fail to live up to the covenant offered to them and sealed by them, the people can still call upon God as the Father who remains steadfast and faithful to the pledge of enduring love. Used relatively infrequently in the Old Testament, the divine name "Father" becomes the predominant way of calling upon God in the New Testament. It is there that the one named "Son," Jesus the Christ, calls upon God as his own Father, and teaches his disciples to call God "Father" (Mt 6:6-14; Lk 11:1-4).

Calling upon God as "Father" by the one called "Son," Jesus the Christ, can be best understood in relation to the stories and dreams of Israel. Since the dawn of creation, the letters of God's unspeakable name have been and are being spelled out. The divine names are being given even as we seek to name God. In story, we receive hints and traces of the divine name. There is the story of Abraham and Isaac (Gn 22). Here is a father who offers what is most precious and most valuable to him, his own life in his son, as a gift to God. Father Abraham surrenders his son Isaac, giving away what is nearest and dearest to him: his own flesh and blood. He has been addressed as an "I" by a "Thou." The gift of what is most precious to him is what is called forth from him. And the return of Father Abraham's giving of life in love and for love is life itself. Isaac lives.

Then there is Jacob who weeps and longs and hurts and hopes for his son (Gn 37ff). Father Jacob pines for his Joseph, the beloved child plotted against and betrayed by Jacob's other sons, the brothers of Joseph. Yet the bonds of love between father and son cannot be broken. Nothing, not even death, can separate what love binds. Even into old age, the father cherishes his son: the one who was sold cheap, betrayed without a second thought, readily turned over by those all too willing to sever love's bond for some small gain. But love endures amidst trial, hardship, and heaviness of heart: a father's love for a son, a son's love for his father. A love once cast into the pit stands forth in its fullness in Joseph who, rising above the snares and entanglements of the darkened and atrophied human heart, forgives his betrayers, his own brothers. Joseph is reunited with his father, whose life is far spent but whose desire for the sight of his son could not be snuffed out over all the years and across the many miles. Love's coming is constant, even at life's end.

These are stories within which God is being named. They give hints or clues; they provide letters by which the name of God is being spelled out. Then and now. As the stories are told and heard, the name of God is being spoken. And we dare to speak to God in response. The stories help us to name God "Father": the One whose name is above all naming, but whose life is love itself, especially for the last, the littlest, and the least; the One whose love is like the love of a mother whose womb quivers at the sight of her child in distress, in pain, in weakness, in vulnerability (Jer 31:20; Ps

22), or like a vigilant mother bear protecting her young cubs from harm (Hos 13:8), or, as in early Christian iconography, a pelican feeding her young.

In the Old Testament, both "Word" and "Wisdom" express God's revealing, creative, saving activity in the world. More specifically, "Word" is God's historical and saving revelation through the prophets. "Spirit" is used with great frequency in the Old Testament, and is roughly approximate to the word "breath." To speak of the Spirit of God is to speak of God's Breath, the very life of God creating, revealing, redeeming. "Word" and "Spirit" express the transcendent God's nearness to the world and, in particular, to the people of the covenant. "Son" is a term found throughout the Old Testament, conveying a rich panoply of meanings. When it is used of Jesus in the New Testament it takes on many of these meanings, but is specifically meant to designate the unique relationship Jesus has with God as his Father.

Speaking of God: New Testament

In the Christian story, those who address God as "Father" do so together with the one who is named "Son," Son of the Father, Jesus the Christ. Jesus names, calls, God "Father," "Abba." This indicates a close, unique relationship of a tender —indeed, intimate—kind, rooted in care and compassion. In learning to speak of and to God, we call God the "Father of Jesus Christ," and we call the Spirit the "Spirit of Jesus Christ." Jesus is named the "Word of God" (Jn 1:1-18), the "Son of God" (Lk 1:35; Mt 3:13-17; Mk 1:9-11; Lk 3:21-22; Jn 1:29-34; Mt 17:5), both "Word" and "Son" in the Spirit.

This is to see and hear the Word of God made flesh in Jesus Christ the Son. He is the expression and gift of divine love or *agape* originating in the Father and poured out into his Body, the church, whose members become in turn expressions and channels of this gift of life, light, and love. Jesus the Son is the Word, the expression of Love without origin who is the Father, as are those who are configured to him in love; the Spirit is Breath, that inner force which makes the Father's expression in Word and its manifold configurations in love possible.

In the baptism of Jesus by John, the Spirit descends upon Jesus, and God's voice is heard: "This is my Son, the Beloved, with whom I am well pleased" (Mt 3:13-17; Mk 1:9-11; Lk 3:21-22). In the waters of the Jordan, Jesus is immersed in the human reality, plunged into the harshness of sin and suffering, which he takes upon himself. He comes out of the waters anointed in the Spirit to speak and to breathe, indeed to be, God's love amidst the starkness and splendor of the human reality, taking upon himself the yoke of sin and death. In the waters of the Jordan we see Christ as the perfect icon of the Father, immersed in sinful humanity and then sent forth as the Son in and by the Spirit, the Breath of God.

Immersed in the fullness of the human reality, anointed by the Spirit of God, Jesus the Son is led by the same Spirit into the treacherous wilderness (Mt 4:1-11; Mk 1:12-13; Lk 4:1-13). There he is alone. He has to face what has to be faced and come to terms with it. Sooner or later we all have to get around to playing the hand we have been dealt. And it is in the desert, the barren place wherein the landscape of the heart becomes a wide open space, that Jesus begins to see more clearly the cards that are his. It is in the desert that each one of us can see the hand we have been dealt.

Soaked, awash in the human reality, he lives with anguish and pain, hunger and sleeplessness. He is tempted. There is the lust for power; the lure of admiration and reputation, recognition and great achievement; the compulsion to do great things solely by force of human effort. And then there are all the seemingly insatiable desires of the heart. In that space called wilderness, the wideness of the human heart, Jesus resists. He faces the darkness and comes through it. The darkness leaves him for a while. But it will return (Lk 4:13).

The Spirit of God is upon Jesus, anointing him as the Father's own Son. He is sent from the darkness to speak a word of light, life, and love to the world—but especially to the last, the littlest, the least, those who have nothing, and so know their need of God, of life, of love. Even and especially in the darkness. The Son is sent, even there, by the Spirit, the Breath of God, to be light, life, and love, to bring good news. And the news is this: "God sent his only Son into the world" (1 Jn 4:9). "God has sent the Spirit of his Son into our hearts" (Gal 4:6). The Spirit is Love's breathing, Love's loving, Life's living, Light's shining. But being in Love, living in Love, is not "toll free." It is a way of living from, toward, and for God the Father through Christ in the Spirit—from the waters of baptism to the table of self-gift in bread and wine, to the vulnerability, passion, dying, and death on the cross—so that the gift can be given yet again in and through his Body, the church.

Compassion's Word

In Christ, the Word in flesh, the human reality has been embraced by Love. He was not ashamed to call us brothers and sisters (Heb 2:11-13), especially in our brokenness and in our vulnerability. Too often, vulnerability is thought to refer to a weakness that places one in a position of being forced to give in indiscriminately to any and all powers and forces. In this view, vulnerability causes one to be adversely affected by persons, events, and circumstances beyond one's control. Properly understood, however, the term describes the fundamental openness of the person to being affected by life, persons, and events. To be human is to be vulnerable, subject to the events and persons that affect us for good or for ill.

At the most fundamental level, human vulnerability is part and parcel of being a person, having a body, being embodied. Our bodies, our selves, are really quite vulnerable in the face of disease, sickness, suffering, accident, and finally death, which claims the life of each human being. No matter how strong a person or a group may be, there are the never-ending reminders that human life is very fragile—a gift—and the forces that bear upon it cannot be predicted or controlled. Whatever precautionary and preventive measures human wisdom may require in order to assure human integrity and flourishing, human beings are fundamentally vulnerable if life is to be lived on life's own terms. This fundamental vulnerability is often overlooked or flatly denied by individuals and by whole societies wherein cults of the young and of youth flourish, where the advertising industry exalts physical perfection and longevity, and where pain, impairment, and limitation are to be avoided at all costs.

Understanding the significance of weakness and vulnerability in the Christian life rests on an appreciation of the weakness and vulnerability of Jesus, Love's Word, particularly in his infancy and in his agony, passion, and death. This mystery is expressed in the *kenosis*, the self-emptying of Jesus Christ first in the Incarnation and then on the cross, whereby he makes himself vulnerable, entering into the condition of human vulnerability as the icon of God's love. The kenotic Christ refused to engage in exercises of authority, power, and control of "the world." Rejecting a type of power that controls and dominates, he embraced instead human weakness and vulnerability. Christ's lordship, his power, is disclosed precisely in his self-emptying.

Jesus' refusal of external "worldly" power and his acceptance of the human condition enabled him to enter the lives of others at their most vulnerable point. This differs greatly from the power of the world. It is the power of a displaced and unknown infant in Bethlehem and a crucified minister and teacher of mercy on Golgotha. The power of *kenosis*, unlike worldly power, manifests itself in vulnerability, care, compassion, self-sacrifice, reciprocity, and mutuality.

To be weak is to stand in need, to be dependent on another, others, and God. It is to recognize that strength, power, indeed life itself, is not of one's own making but is the gracious gift of the creator of all creatures. To accept and celebrate one's life as a creature involves an admission that one cannot exist independently of others and God, and that one stands in need of them for any growth and development.

Vulnerability may be understood as the capacity to be open, to be attracted, touched, or moved by the draw of God's love as this is experienced in one's own life or in the lives of others. It is vulnerability that enables one to enter into relationships of interpersonal communication and communion with others who recognize their own weakness and need. Vulnerability requires the integrity and the strength—indeed, the power—to risk enormous pain, to bear the burdens of the darkest hour without avoidance, denial, deception. It demands the stamina to be open in order to be touched in one's fragility. Vulnerability implies a willingness to lose oneself, to be knocked off center by the claim of the other upon one in the hope of finding one's true self. It demands the readiness to die to one's self so that one might truly live.

In Jesus Christ, Love's Word, we see in a fleshly way the compassion of the Father. The term "compassion" refers to the very core of one's deepest feelings—to what we usually think of as the heart. The Hebrew word for "compassion" expresses the empathetic attachment of one being to another. This feeling of attachment is experienced by mothers; it is experienced in the bowels, the entrails, or, in common parlance, the guts. The Hebrew word for a woman's womb and the word for compassion are related, and both are related to the word for mercy. Thus, the mother's intimate, physical relationship with her newborn is the prime image for compassion and, hence, the compassion of God in Christ. To speak of the compassion of God is to speak of God's quivering womb—a womb that trembles at the sight of the frailty, suffering, and weakness of the child. The mother's physical and psychological bond with her child provides a basis for the development of our understanding of compassion and related notions of the pity, mercy, and tenderness of God. Indeed, the Council of Toledo in 675 A.D. spoke of the "womb of the Father."

In this light, compassion may be understood as the capacity to be attracted and moved by the fragility, weakness, and suffering of another. It is the ability to be vulnerable enough to undergo risk and loss for the good of the other. Compassion involves a movement toward the other to be of assistance. But it also entails a movement of participation in the experience of the other in order to be present and available in solidarity and communion. Compassion requires sensitivity to what is weak and wounded as well as the vulnerability to be affected by the pain of the other. It also demands action to alleviate pain and suffering. One's deepest inner feelings of compassion are to find expression in acts of compassion, mercy, and kindness.

Though this image for compassion is a maternal one, compassion is not to be understood as exclusive to mothers or women, or even as more natural to them than to men. Compassion also springs from the heart of a father, as in Psalm 103:13: "As a father has compassion for his children; so the Lord has compassion for those who fear him"; or from the heart of a brother, as in Genesis 43:30, where Joseph is overcome with affection for his younger brother Benjamin. Compassion is tenderness readily moved to action. It is action that seeks to heal in the face of tragedy, to extend forgiveness for offenses. In the New Testament, Jesus embodies God's compassion in his preaching and healing; in his concern for lost humanity; and in his self-sacrificial love on the cross. The followers of Jesus are to live lives of compassion impelled by the Spirit, the Breath of God.

Abundant Mercy

Jesus provided prime examples of compassion, notably in the parable of the Good Samaritan who had compassion on the wounded traveler, but especially in the parable of the Prodigal Son whose father sees him in the distance and, moved with compassion, runs to meet him.

The story of the father of two sons (Lk 15:11ff) bespeaks the Son's knowledge of the superabundance of the Father's love. In common sense language, this is a story of a good boy and a bad boy. And it is a story of a father who appears to like badness rather than goodness—or at least to reward the bad boy and overlook the good one, because the good boy doesn't seem to get a fair shake. He has played by the rules. He has paid his dues. But who wins favor with the father? Not the one who stays home and takes care of business. Rather, it is the son who takes off and squanders the goods who receives the father's gift of outpouring, superabundant love.

We see a father waiting. A beloved son has gone wandering and has lost his way. He has distanced himself and is nowhere in sight. The father's heart aches. It hurts. And then a love that has squandered even the very gift of love is brought low enough to see the bottomlessness of love's abundance. Hoping for just a small taste of it, he returns. To love. To the father. To his father: the one who waits and embraces, who relishes, delights in, and celebrates the return of love's gift come back as a gift. Gift through and through. The life thought to be lost and beyond retrieval has come back. Love, come again!

The good boy, the one who plays by the rules and anticipates being rewarded for his good behavior, cannot fathom it: the utter gratuity of love's giving—giving as gift rather than as reward; pouring life forth freely and without cost, not as a payback for a deed well done. This is precisely what the bad boy receives. He stands naked and disheveled, shivering and dirty-mouthed from eating pig food, empty handed and brokenhearted before his father. He knows his need. It is in his need, rather than in his abundance, that he turns himself over to his father, holding on only to a thin thread of hope that he might be given a small sip of mercy. And he receives more than he could ever imagine, as gift. Sheer gratuity.

The story of the father of two sons is a word of unrestricted forgiveness and superabundant mercy—a prodigious love. It is for those who recognize their need, rather than their self-sufficiency. But it is also for those who have the haunting suspicion that all our projects and plans and causes and efforts, no matter how noble and worthy, do not earn us what the heart really longs for: Love, the life that pours itself forth. Love given freely. Love that cannot be earned, but can only be given—and received, as the son receives from the abundance of his father's giving.

Attending to the story of the father of two sons, we are awakened afresh to new insight. Our understandings and expectations of fairness and justice are overturned. Our ways of viewing fathers and fatherhood, as well as sons and sonship, are likewise called into question. In telling the story of the two sons, Jesus proposes a radically new understanding of fatherhood, one that is considerably different from prevailing views in the culture of his day. Such a fresh view of the father, rather than reinforcing the patriarchal structures of Jesus' time, poses a challenge to them, because it would have been inconceivable that the son who safeguards the patrimony should be overlooked, while the son who squandered it be celebrated. The fatherhood of patriarchy, and related notions of power, righteousness, and justice, are taken up and turned inside out by the excess of self-emptying love which reaches out and gathers in what is lost and farthest from reach. All the other sheep are left behind by the good shepherd on the hunt for the lost one (Lk 15:1-7; Mt 18:10-14). One coin is so precious that the whole house is overturned in search of it (Lk 15:8-10). A compassionate Samaritan (Lk 10:29-37) defies all expectations by reaching out and coming to the aid of the stranger, indeed the enemy. Not only does he care for the beaten and bedraggled stranger, but he makes provision for him far in excess of what is judged necessary. He does so freely, and without concern for repayment. The owner of the vineyard (Mt 20:1-16) demonstrates a generosity that defies logic. It is the logic of the gift: given freely, without cost, regardless of effort, prescinding from considerations of merit.

Calling on God as "Father," we place ourselves alongside the son known as the Prodigal. Like him, we often find ourselves living with dashed hopes and failed promises. Our lives are marked, sometimes scarred, by an unpredictable but steady flow of interruptions. At times we feel swallowed up in random cycles of disorder and disintegration, with ever-so-brief respites of order and tranquillity. Then, often with no logical or rational cause, we are knocked out of order into disorder and disarray again. And then again. Naming God "Father" demands that we name the disorder and disorientation out of which we speak, not just as individual persons, but as communities, as whole peoples. Calling on God as "Father" demands that we bring to speech the harshness of the human reality, the unspeakable horror of evil and suffering in our world, praying together with the poor and weak and wounded who suffer the greatest burden in our time. With the Prodigal we call upon the Father with those who do not share in the world's gains, those outside the compass of plenty, the ones who even this day eat scraps.

Like the Prodigal we must take stock of the squalor in which we live, a shambles often of our own making, and begin to speak the name of the Father in its midst. It is often only when we drink from the dregs that we find the strength to call upon God, to start the long journey back to the Father. And in that gaze from afar, we are recognized as the daughter who is the end of God's rainbow, the apple of God's eye, the son in whom the Father takes great pride and pleasure.

Fleshly Love: Incarnation and the Cross

Christian faith affirms that pure Love without source is expressed in Jesus who is named "Word" and "Son," and in Love's Breath named "Spirit." Jesus speaks in a fleshly way the compassion of God, the one he called "Father." In Christ, the Word in flesh, the love of God enters into creation, into the fabric of human life in all its limits, frailty, contingency, tragedy. Following Jesus requires that we accept the invitation to a life of mercy and forgiveness, that we live in relationship with others and God in such a way that we are both vulnerable and compassionate as was Love's Word Jesus, speaking and breathing God's own gift of life and love named "Spirit."

Love's speaking and breathing is enfleshed through the Incarnation and in the cross of Christ. Here we see and are invited to participate in the self-giving of God in love, living in and from this gift, realizing that this, rather than prevailing views of power and success, is what transforms human life, history, the world. The cross is our assurance that we participate in the life and glory of God not by avoiding or bypassing the negative experiences of our lives, but by entering into and growing through them. This is the central meaning and message of the cross of Christ: light shines amidst darkness; life emerges from death; love prevails over all evil.

Immersed in the waters of the Jordan and the fullness of the human reality, Jesus is plunged into that wide darkness of the heart's wilderness. He is brought through by the Breath of Love to be Love itself: Love's gift, Love's Word. But at the end of the day, on the night before he died, Love's giving required yet more. To assure that his own self-giving would continue, that the gift would be given again and yet again, he took the simple earthly realities of bread and wine of the meal and, in and through them, gave himself again: Take and eat. Take and drink (Mt 26:26-29; Mk 14:22-25; Lk 22:14-20; 1 Cor 11:23-26).

His body is given and his blood poured forth in the earthly realities of bread and wine. This is what Love is and does. It pours itself forth, in simple gifts of the earth: bread, wine, water, oil. And it pours itself into the human heart, that land of deep and lasting desire, the land of longing, of an absence aching for light, for life, for love. The heart is the region of wound and wisdom, the Spirit's dwelling within, the place from which Love speaks Love's name, "Father," in and through the Spirit, Love's Breath. This is the Spirit: God's life pouring itself forth, speaking within our hearts, with hope in the midst of darkness and travail. It is the same Spirit pouring itself forth in a cup of cold water given in Christ's name, and in the soothing waters poured from an earthen pitcher to cleanse the feet of those who stand in need. Love pours itself forth in the tending of wounds, in as simple an act as feeding the hungry mouths of children, in staying just a little longer with the aged or infirm, in bearing a sister's burden, in listening long and lovingly when I have nothing more to give to the one who is most in need. It is the same Spirit impelling us to prepare ourselves to have our own feet washed, our own hearts cleansed, our own minds and hearts enlightened, enlivened, guided, healed as a gift which is all the more full in the giving of it.

The cross of Christ is the unsurpassable promise of the divine presence amidst the human reality. Human life, all of it, is the precinct of epiphany—of God's showing, of God's constant speaking and breathing. But nowhere is this presence more resplendent than in our utter poverty. The suffering, passion, and dying of Christ on the cross is Love's Word: giving of itself even and especially in weakness and vulnerability, in darkness and in death. The Love that brought him from the waters of the Jordan through wilderness and the wilds of city streets, then to the supper of self-giving, and finally to the outstretching of his life in giving on the cross, did not leave him then—in the last hour, at that final moment. And the Love that has brought us this far in love, wherever that may be, will not leave us then, in our final hour.

Love's Breath

After his baptism by John, Jesus is driven immediately into the desert by the Spirit in order to contend with Satan. This same Spirit is called, named, the "Spirit of Jesus Christ" when poured out as gift/ing into his Body, the church, at Pentecost. The Spirit is an inner driving force impelling us and keeping us united in love with God, with the world, with each other. This life-giving, Love-breathing Spirit of Jesus enables us to be free from the law of sin (Rom 7) and to live in, with, and from the gift of the freedom of the children of God (Rom 8). The Spirit given to us drives out fear and enables us to address God with Christ, as "Abba." It confirms us in our faith in Jesus Christ, Son of the Father, and makes of us brothers and sisters in Christ, sons and daughters of God. It enables us in this faith and in hope to overcome every obstacle and to remain firm in our witness. It unites us with the whole of creation in its travail. It teaches us to pray, even when we do not know how or what to pray.

We stand as brothers and sisters to the one who is named "Son of God," "Word of God," both "Son" and "Word" in the Spirit. With him, we are sons and daughters of God the Father. Those who call upon God as Father "from the inside out," from a heart steeped in prayer, know that what is given to us cannot be repaid, or returned in kind. All our efforts at response are possible only because we have first been given a gift. Like the letters on a page, or the words of our tongues which seek to sing God's praise, they spring forth as response because they have first and finally been given to us.

In the Christian story, "I" have been summoned by a "Thou," a "You" who is not just active in history and present to creation, but who is near, whose life is expressed, poured forth in the Word who is Jesus, Son of the living God, the Word whispering in Love's breathing within my deepest parts, within the heart of each human being. Being named a "child of God" is possible because of the language of Father and Son. This language, this act of self-expressing, we call "Spirit," "Spirit of God," "Holy Spirit," the "Spirit of Our Lord Jesus Christ." This is the Love within which I am recognized and addressed as an "I" in my deepmost self, the heart. Receiving this Love in the depths of the heart elicits a response: "Thou," "You," my "Father"—overspilling Love-in-excess—sheer gift given to this child, this daughter, this son. "Because you are children, God has sent the Spirit of his Son into our hearts, crying, 'Abba! Father!' So you are no longer a slave but a child, and if a child then also an heir, through God" (Gal 4:6-7).

Our first response to gift is not to respond, but to receive. And then, without burden of cost or interest, to live freely with, in, and from the gift. This is what is ours through Jesus Christ the Son, the Father's perfect image and likeness in his self-gift at the supper and on the cross, and in the Spirit alive in our hearts crying out in hope. Seized and saturated by Love's outpouring, addressed by Word and in Spirit,

Love's speaking and breathing, living and loving among us, we dare to speak back Love's name: Our Father.

Father, Son, Spirit: In Loving Relation

"Father" is not God's proper name. Nor is "God" God's name. God has no proper name. "Father," "Son," "Spirit" are names that designate relationships rather than who God is in God's fullness. God is inexhaustible mystery. Unfathomable. But through the process of naming, the three names "Father," "Son," and "Spirit" emerge in relation to one another *and* to us. They bespeak the profoundly relational character of the divine mystery, the One whose name is beyond all naming: "God is love" (1 Jn 4:8).

What is this strange and elusive thing we call love? Quite simply, it is life pouring itself forth. To say that "God is love" is to say that God is not enclosed, turned in on self. God is the life that pours itself forth: constantly, abundantly, excessively, never-to-stop-coming-as-gift. Life is altogether and absolutely gift: a gift come freely, unexpectedly, undeservedly. This gift is constant, trustworthy, faithful. God who is always and everywhere pouring forth is faithful.

Calling God "Father" is a way of naming our relationship to God, a way of responding to the gift of Love expressed in the Word who is the Son of the Father, breathing life and love in the Spirit. It is our way of naming and celebrating the gift received, and of entering into relationship with the Source of life giving itself forth as gift in every instant. This unfathomable mystery of life pouring itself forth is as much Mother as Father, while at the same time neither

Father nor Mother. But in the naming of God which takes place within the Christian story, this Pure Source of Love without beginning or end is named "Father" of the Son Jesus Christ, Our Lord, whose Spirit is given to us so that we might speak and breathe Love's Word in our own time and place.

CHAPTER TWO

A Grammar of Gift:
The Doctrine of the Trinity

T HE TRINITY IS THE CENTRAL MYSTERY of Christian faith and life. It is the source of all the other mysteries of Christian faith, the light that enlightens them (*Catechism of the Catholic Church*, 234). But, all too often, talk about the Trinity takes the form of lofty speech rather than plain words. If the Trinity is obscured rather than disclosed by the way it is spoken of, then how are we to live the fullness of the Christian life to which speech about the Trinity is intended to invite us? How are we to understand all the other mysteries of the Christian faith that the doctrine of the Trinity enlightens if, in fact, we are cloudy rather than clear about the central Christian mystery?

As a child I was confused rather than delighted by drawings in catechisms and books about the saints that depicted the Trinity as a perfect triangle. There was often an old white-bearded man at the top, with the white-robed sandy-haired Jesus on one side and a white dove representing the Holy Spirit on the other side. And I can recall being perplexed and discouraged in my early ruminations about what all this might mean. I was vexed rather than comforted by images of the Trinity—most of which conveyed a sense of the inscrutability of this supreme mystery.

At the same time, I was drawn to the Trinity, perhaps precisely because it was presented to me as the loftiest, the highest of the Christian mysteries. It was all the more attractive because I was told that no mind could take it in, since it is simply beyond the beyond. Attempting to do so would be like trying to fit the ocean into a child's sand bucket. Nonetheless I tried! Perhaps I still do—although as an adult I have come to the deeper realization that it is the mystery that enfolds us, rather than we who comprehend it by way of the mind's acumen. Even when I was a boy, however, it was altogether clear to me that if it is indeed true that the Trinity is the highest, loftiest Christian mystery, then it must make some kind of sense. That conviction has never left me.

I also remember clearly that as a grade school student I was told that one should not pray to the Trinity, but to Jesus. The Trinity, I was told, is an idea, a concept. You don't pray *to* the Trinity. But over the years I have come to learn that Christian prayer is Trinitarian: to the Father, through the Son, in the Spirit.

Christian faith is Trinitarian faith. Christian life is Trinitarian life. And Christian spirituality is Trinitarian spirituality. Yet most who profess the Christian faith would be hard pressed to explain what is meant by the word "Trinity," to say nothing of the truth about God which the Trinitarian doctrine seeks to express. The response, far too often, is "It's a mystery." This may be followed by the story of the boy at the seaside with his bucket.

Speaking of Mystery

One of the most important things in life is learning how not to know. This is not the same as simply not knowing. What is meant by "not to know" here involves admitting, accepting, and embracing our limits. One of the first things we need to learn in our approach to God is that in our relationship to God we must embrace the tensive interaction between knowing and not knowing. God is not to be known through the power of the intelligence. But the God whose very being is Love in superabundant gift can be glimpsed, tasted, pursued in the desire of the human heart which longs in love for Love itself. Our attempts to speak of the mystery of God can commence in earnest only after we accept that our stumbling does not cease, but is ongoing. We are never quite successful in our effort to seek or speak of God in terms that are clearly intelligible, by way of definitions that are watertight and hermetically sealed. What is to be known of God is to be known in prayer, that is, in a disposition of contemplative receptivity, of poised spiritual liberty, in which the gift of love and light is given. God will not be seized by rational analysis, or by techniques of any sort, no matter how religious or pious they might be.

Mystery often implies a sense of unintelligibility bordering on nonsense. But real mystery is that which invites and allures us into fuller participation, all the while exceeding our want to grasp it, hold on to it, contain it. Indeed, in much the same way, human love is a mystery. We are invited, at times allured, by another. Something in us is touched, moved, drawn by the other. The closer we come, and the more we grow in love, the clearer it becomes that the beloved cannot be tied down, grasped, defined once and for all. Mystery is not something that is unintelligible. In terms of the original biblical image, mystery is a plan which a king shares only with his closest advisors. Thus the big picture of the mystery is known by the king, and to some degree by those to whom he discloses it, but not necessarily by all who are affected by it. Mystery, even the divine mystery, is not a mathematical puzzle bordering on absurdity.

From the perspective of Christian faith, God's plan has been disclosed in the Word through the presence and power of the Spirit. In this sense the Trinity is mystery. What is most mysterious is God's superabundant life pouring itself forth, the love of God who gives and gives again but is never emptied in the giving. This self-giving is at the very heart of who God is. The incomprehensibility of God lies in the utter gratuity of life and love, in God's constant coming as gift. God is inexhaustible Gift, Given and Gift/ing in and through love. This is who God is and how God is. Whatever may be known of this ineffable mystery, unfathomable because of the depth and prodigality of this life pouring itself forth in love, is known in and through the gift of the indwelling Spirit of God enabling us to recognize the Word made flesh whose life, passion, death, and Resurrection are the very disclosure of God's mystery. The life, suffering, death, and Resurrection of Jesus bespeak, reveal, God's self-giving as gift. Mystery is always more, always ahead of us, inviting us to greater life, light, and love. When we pray and engage in spiritual disciplines, most of us do not look *at* God, but rather look *for*

God, constantly seeking precisely because our lives are *in via*, on the way to fuller participation in mystery.

Our grammar, our way of speaking of God as Father, Son, and Spirit, is intended to invite meaningful and truthful communication about God as well as participation in the mystery about which this language speaks. In speaking the language, it is not so much that we grasp the mystery but that we open ourselves so as to be grasped by it. The grammar of the Trinity is meant to convey the simply astonishing truth: "God is love" (1 Jn 4:8). God's Word is spoken; God's Spirit is poured forth. The life and love of God are not past tense, but present, ecstatic, alive, outreaching, gift/ing here and now.

Lofty Language?

Many contemporary theologies of the Trinity point out that all too often the doctrine of the Trinity has been and continues to be far removed from the life of ordinary Christians. For most, the teaching about the Trinity is ethereal, lofty, removed from the realm of everyday concerns and day-in-day-out living. The doctrine seems to have little or no bearing on the way ordinary Christians actually strive to live out their commitments. If it is thought of at all in any sustained or systematic fashion, the Trinity is often judged to have little practical consequence. Even while the doctrine is said to be central to Christian faith, it is lamentably quite marginal to the lives of ordinary Christians trying to live out their faith in a highly complex world.

While it may be true that the doctrine of the Trinity is marginal to the faith and life of the vast number of Christians, an awareness of the mystery of God's superabundant love which speech about the Father, Son, and Spirit seeks to convey could be more central than it may appear at first glance. While the teaching about the Trinity, or the Trinitarian doctrine, may be dismissed as a vexing puzzle by many, in the ordinary lives of the Christian faithful there is indeed some grasp of the mystery which the doctrine seeks to express. In other words, there is often a deep experience of the Father as the originator and Pure Source of Love, Jesus Christ the Son who is that Love seen and heard in Word, and the Spirit as the ongoing and inexhaustible activity of that Love, drawing everything and everyone back to the origin and end of Love in the bonding of Love itself. This might be referred to as the Trinitarian nature of Christian faith and experience, which may or may not be articulated in the more precise language of the Trinitarian doctrine.

In much the same way that a person learns to speak and understand a language long before the rules of grammar are mastered, many speak and understand the fundamental meanings communicated in Trinitarian grammar, the language of Father, Son, and Spirit, without comprehending the rules of grammar, that is, the doctrine of the Trinity. We recognize the figure in the gospels called "Christ" or "Son" or "Word" only because of the gift of the Holy Spirit dwelling in our hearts. What we see and hear in him is not just him but the One, the Father, who sent him (Jn 14). In works of art we catch a glimpse of the Father, Son, and Spirit, and in poems, in hymns, in acts of praise and prayers of petition, we call upon them. We are plunged into the waters of life "in the name of the Father, and of the Son, and of the Holy Spirit." We mark ourselves with the sign of the cross in the same name, demonstrating our belief that it is in the dying and rising of Christ that Love itself is given and gift/ing. Sunday by Sunday, or day by day, we gather in the Spirit at the table of the Lord to receive and celebrate the gift of the Body and Blood of the Lord, becoming configurations of the Word in flesh, ongoing expressions of the creative action of the Spirit in the church and in the world. Our prayer is addressed to the Father, through, with, and in Christ, in the communion of the Holy Spirit.

If we are unsettled by questions about whether Jesus is really God or if the Spirit is equal to the Father, there are answers in the doctrine of the Trinity, the rules of grammar by which we seek and probe and dare to speak of the divine mystery. But these questions, and their answers, are not the bread and butter of Christian faith. It is in the practice of Christian faith and living, in the doxology of the human heart praising God in the name of Father, Son, and Spirit, that we receive, acknowledge, and respond to the mystery of the Trinity. When we are at home with the faith and practice of the church, Trinity is the language spoken, the language of the house.

The word "Trinity" is not found in the Creed which we profess week by week. But it is altogether Trinitarian in structure: We believe in God the Father, we believe in Jesus Christ the Son, we believe in the Holy Spirit the Lord, the giver of life. With the Father and the Son, the Spirit is worshiped and glorified. Christian faith is a beholding of the mystery of Love's Pure Source, expressed and expressing in Word and Spirit. These three are related to one another and to us, inviting our participation in the divine life, which is a communion in the one Love. The doctrine of the Trinity provides the rules of grammar by which we seek to understand and communicate as clearly as possible the mystery of outpouring and undying Love, Love without origin or end, the mystery of God who is Giver, Given, and Gift/ing.

Learning the Rules of Grammar

Anyone who has studied the rules of grammar—whether of one's own language or of a foreign one—knows firsthand that appreciation of a language and the ability to live and communicate within it can only be enhanced by understanding grammar. Grammar has to do with a way of speaking correctly. Rules of grammar set the limits within which creative discourse can take place. Rules of grammar do not guarantee that we will speak the truth, but if we are to speak in a meaningful and coherent way, we must work within the rules of grammar. For example, early on in our speaking we learn the rule that a singular subject requires a singular verb. A grammar sets out rules of speaking meaningfully in the search for truth.

The experience of countless Christian missionaries may serve as an example of the way in which rules of grammar are discerned. One of the great contributions of these missionaries has been the production of various grammatical texts, books containing the rules of grammar, the way of speaking correctly, for indigenous peoples. Upon arrival in distant lands to spread the gospel, one of the first tasks the missionaries undertook was to listen to the language of the Zulu people in Africa, or the Inuit in the northernmost parts of North America, or the Taureg in North Africa. They sought to hear what was being said, and to listen to the way in which it was said. Only then could they determine and set down rules of grammar, that is, the rules by which the people and the missionaries could speak to one another in meaningful and intelligible ways.

In a similar way, the doctrine of the Trinity contains rules of grammar by which we speak meaningfully of the self-giving God whose name above all names is Love. The doctrine of the Trinity is a grammar of gift. As such, not only does a Trinitarian grammar have rules within which meaningful speech about God can be conducted, it also makes possible a form of liminal discourse, speech at the edge of comprehension, since what is spoken of eludes our grasp. The Trinitarian doctrine, a grammar of gift, enables us to hear more precisely and respond somewhat more adequately to the language of self-giving which is the very ineffability of the mystery of God named "Father, Son, and Spirit."

To Speak Rightly of Love

How and why did speaking of God in accord with an explicitly Trinitarian grammar develop? How and why did the experience of God through Christ the Word made flesh by the Holy Spirit come to be formulated in terms that can sound so lofty, abstract, removed, distant, theoretical—terms such as three "persons" in one "nature"? Answering these questions may help us understand more clearly the mystery expressed in Trinitarian language, enabling us to live a Christian spirituality which is more consciously Trinitarian through and through, and to participate more fully in the life of the three in one Love—a profoundly relational mystery.

The doctrine of the Trinity originated in an effort to think through the implications of Christ's role and the Spirit's role in our salvation. Though it may not seem so today, this was a very practical concern for the early church. The Old Testament and the New Testament convey a rich complex of images and stories through which we learn to speak of God: Father, Son, Spirit. Because in scripture the divine names are disclosed through speech that is abundant, metaphorical, poetic, and imaginative, there emerged a need to specify more clearly the way in which these names are to be used in speaking meaningfully of God. The formulation of the Trinitarian doctrine involved a search for rules of speech that affirms truth. The Trinitarian grammar does not disclose the fullness of the divine mystery, but it does set the parameters of discourse by which the truth may be sought. Although later theological investigations into the Trinity develop the grammar further, they rely on the rules of grammar in the Trinitarian doctrine to ensure that creative speculation respects and does not violate the doctrinal. This is to say that all further theological speculation on the Trinity must work within the rules of grammar set in the doctrine.

In early Christian history, questions began to emerge about the relationship between Jesus, the Lord (*kyrios*) (Phil 2:11) and the one he called "Father." Jesus was understood to be the perfect image (*eikon*) of the invisible God in whom everything has been created (Col 1:15-16), the eternal Word (*logos*) of God become flesh (Jn 1:14). This belief gave rise to the question of whether Jesus the Christ shares in God's nature, is of the same "stuff" or substance as God.

But early Christian reflection remained focused on God's saving activity in history, on what God had done in and through Jesus the Lord and the gift of the Holy Spirit. This creative, saving, sanctifying action of Father, Son, and Spirit constitutes the *oikonomia*, the "economy" of salvation. The *oikonomia* was the central concern of early Christian theology, beholding what God had done in history through the sending of the Son and the gift of the life-giving Spirit, proclaimed and handed on in the scriptures and in the living traditions of Christian communities.

To understand the grammar of the Trinity it is necessary to understand the move from the poetic to the propositional, from the abundance of scriptural images and metaphors for God, such as shepherd, rock, fortress, to more precise ideas. In learning to speak rightly of God it is necessary to enunciate truth in clear concepts. The Trinitarian doctrine sets forth rules for seeking propositional clarity. One of the purposes of doctrine is to be clear about the ideas put forward, appealing more to intellect and understanding than to affect.

In the history of the doctrine of the Trinity, it is important to see the enunciation of the doctrine and the setting of the rules of grammar first in the Creed. The format of the Creed is to repeat what is known from scripture about Father, Son, and Spirit, doing so in such a way as to formulate a grammar. What is affirmed is the distinction and activity of the three who are God. This is given more precision with the use of the term *ousia* or "substance," to make sure that all three together are considered fully God so that the divine character of the redemptive and sanctifying work of Father, Son, and Spirit is assured. On the other hand, to assure distinction among the three, the Greeks used the word *hypostasis* and the Latins *persona*. At the risk of oversimplification, in early Christian centuries "person" named what is distinct in God, without defining specifically what is meant by this. "Substance" named what is common to Father, Son, and Spirit, because of the conviction that in speaking of God what is said of the Father's divinity is to be said of the Son and, later, of the Spirit.

Hence, a Trinitarian grammar, the correct way of speaking of God the Father, Son, and Spirit, will say that the Son is God by nature, and person in his distinction from the Father, and the Spirit is God by nature, and person in being distinct from the Father and the Son. This is located first in the work of the economy of salvation, so as to assure that the activities associated with Son and Spirit are seen as divine activities, not those of lesser beings.

There is then a shift to explain how this is so within the mystery of God, and not just in the works of Father, Son, and Spirit. Further, the question of whether God did truly dwell on earth, whether Jesus Christ is the same as God, the one he called "Father," and other questions about how the suffering of Jesus Christ could be reconciled with a perfect, unchanging, imperishable God, could be answered only in more speculative fashion, through philosophical categories, in metaphysical language. This speculative turn in answer to questions of the equality of Christ to God, and the question of whether God suffers, resulted in giving somewhat less attention to God's saving acts in history through Word and Spirit, and more attention to the precise nature of the relationship of Father, Son, and Spirit to one another. This tension in early Christian theology between the attention given to the works of Father, Son, and Spirit in the economy of salvation and the attention given to the mystery within the God-head persists even today. It serves as a reminder that it is in knowing the Father, Son, and Spirit that we know God, and that we should not start with a notion of the divinity and then apply the grammar of the Trinity to it. All theology, in-deed, all Christian faith and practice, has to start with the economic Trinity, with the naming of Father, Son, and Spirit in the scriptures. The answer to theology's single most im-portant question—Who is God?—emerges by looking to God's grand economy of redemption through Word and Spirit in history, and then reads this back into the mystery of God as Love itself. This is crucial in understanding a Trini-tarian spirituality, for participation in the economy of salva-tion is a participation in the very life of God. Through such participation we are engaged in the gift and task of deifica-tion, sharing in the divine life.

In short, the earliest Christian theological reflection was concerned with God's salvation in Jesus Christ through the continuing presence and power of the Holy Spirit in the church and in the world. When tough and sticky questions emerged, answers were sought on metaphysical grounds, in philosophical terms. But *theologia*, that is, more speculative considerations about the mystery of God, must always remain rooted in the *oikonomia*, in the creative, saving, sanctifying ac-tion of Father, Son, and Spirit in the economy of salvation. When the focus on the *oikonomia* is clear and sharp, the dis-tinction between Father, Son, and Spirit is located in creating, saving, and sanctifying works. When the focus is on *theologia*, the distinction is sought within the Godhead and expressed as a relation between the three in one divine nature.

Three in the One Love

In setting the rules of the grammar of the Trinity, two key terms emerge in speaking of God: "person" and "substance" or "nature." "Person" names what is distinct; "substance" or "nature" names what is common to the three. It is a facile reading of a complex matter to suggest that in the Christian East "person" is given priority, while in the Christian West, the emphasis on "substance," or oneness, eclipses the distinctiveness of the three in the economy of salvation. In all early Christian reflection, primacy was given to the distinctiveness and uniqueness of Spirit, Son, and Father in the economy of redemption: each one, distinct in relation, shares in God's life and partakes of the one divine nature. In the traditions of both East and West, attention is given to the Word and the Spirit in the economy of redemption, to the diversity and uniqueness of the three persons within the oneness, the equality which is theirs by virtue of sharing the divine nature. The Trinity is first and finally a mystery of Father, Son, and Spirit—three in the one Love. The Father speaks a Word and breathes Love, drawing us into communion with the one Love. God is not turned inward, but is toward us, for us, with us, in us. God relates to us as Father, Son, and Spirit, distinct in their relations. This is what we mean when we say that there are three in the one Love.

In charting out the rules of grammar, the term "person" was used simply to mean a distinct one, a distinct subject, without further explanation at first as to what is meant by subject. To explain this further, Scholastic theology used the concept of relationality to define divine person. The use of the term "person" was and is not intended to convey that there are three different consciousnesses or three separate wills in God. Nor does it mean that there is a separation of consciousness and free subjectivity over against one another. Unlike human persons, the divine persons are not individual centers of consciousness. In using "person" when speaking of God, and in saying that there are three "persons" in the one Love, the relational is both unique and crucial, because being person in God is defined only in and through relationship with the others: Father, Son, Spirit are persons in and through their relations.

Being person in this sense is not being an individuated center of consciousness, a free reigning subjectivity exercised in individual acts of knowing and willing. Rather, "person" is always "being toward" another, for the other, in relation. To say that there are "three persons" in God, that is, that God is Father, Son, and Spirit, is a way of naming what is unique or different in God, what is distinct precisely in relation. To say that there are three persons in God is to say that God is not an in-and-of-itself, a for-itself, or a by-itself. The term "person" when used of God is a way of saying that God is always toward and for the other in the self-giving which is constitutive of love. Self-giving is always in relation to another, to others. The distinctive manner of self-giving varies by virtue of the uniqueness of the relation of Father, Son, and Spirit; Giver, Given, and Gift/ing.

Through the grammar of the Trinity we seek to speak with greater precision about Father, Son, Spirit, three persons in loving eternal communion. But the purpose of such speech is to invite us into the depth of relations at the heart of the mystery of God. The three are not the same, but distinct precisely in their relations: three in one Love. All of this is an attempt to say that it is the very being of God to be in relation. God is not a self-contained self, but One whose very being is constituted by the relations of interpersonal love. What the Trinitarian doctrine seeks to throw light on is the altogether relational character of the Love who loves in and through pouring life forth for the other. It is a grammar of gift, helping to clarify the parameters within which we speak of God as Giver, Given, Gift/ing. By the Spirit who is Gift/ing, dwelling within our hearts, we behold the mystery of the Trinity in the Incarnate Word, Given, whose life, words, mission, passion, dying, and rising are the very love of the Giver of all life and love.

In the grammar of the Trinity, attention must always be given to the diversity, uniqueness, particularity of the three. But the three are in one Love, thus calling for attention to oneness, to what is had in common. The rules of the grammar allow for speech about uniqueness-diversity as well as sameness-oneness, about three *hypostases* (persons) distinct in their relations as well as about one shared *ousia* (nature or substance).

Giver, Given, Gift/ing

A revitalized understanding of the Trinity rooted in the biblical, creedal, and liturgical traditions favors an emphasis on persons (*hypostases*) in relationship and communion, in contrast to substance (*ousia*). There is a new focus on divine works in explaining the mystery of the Trinity. Often this avoids speculation on the intradivine nature, the mystery within the Godhead, and attends to things the way they are, i.e., the Triune God as creating, redeeming, sanctifying, thus giving us a share in the divine life. In such perspective, the primary and ultimate category of being—everything that is— is relational. The mystery of the Word become flesh in the Incarnation, the relationship of Son to Father and of Spirit to Father and Son, discloses the very life of God as well as the destiny of everything created in God's image—to be brought into the communion in one Love. All reality is personal, that is, *toward* and *for.* God is self-giving, outpouring, ecstatic Love. God is not foremost a self-contained individual. God is personal. How do we know this? We know it because of the way that God is for us in the grand economy of salvation: Father, Son, and Spirit—toward us, for us, with us, in us as Giver, Given, and Gift/ing.

Understanding the doctrine of the Trinity as a grammar of gift requires attention to small words, terms that are often overlooked—the prepositions. These are the most important words of the grammar, because they express relationship. Often understood to be defined propositionally, in terms of clear concepts, it may be more accurate to say that Christian faith is defined prepositionally, since prepositions express sheer relation. These small words define the relationship of Father, Son, and Spirit, the relationship of the three in one Love to us, and our relationship with God. Christian life is always *to* the Father, *through* the Son, *in* the Spirit. We make the sign of the cross *in* the name *of* the Father, and *of* the Son, and *of* the Holy Spirit, and pray *to* the Father, *through* the Son, *in* the Spirit. In the church's liturgical life, prayer is addressed *to* the Father, *through*, *with*, and *in* Christ, *in* the unity of the Holy Spirit. And at the heart of the Trinitarian doctrine there is the belief that God is *with* us, *for* us, *in* us.

The doctrine of the Trinity affirms that God is committed to humanity and its history; that God's covenant with us is irrevocable; that God's face is immutably turned toward us in love; that God's presence to us is utterly reliable and constant. The basis for these affirmations is the self-revelation of God in the economy of salvation, specifically, for Christians, in what is revealed through Jesus Christ and the gift of the Spirit. Christian faith is the Spirit-assisted response to the Incarnate Word of God, Jesus Christ, who reveals the face of the invisible God. This God is personal, that is, intrinsically related. God does not exist as an isolated being-turned-in-on-itself. God is always toward the other, toward us, for us.

Since human beings are created in the image of an inherently relational God, we are not created as selves in isolation. Rather, we are who we are and come to be what we are called to be in and through our relationships with other persons. In the Incarnate Word and through the indwelling Spirit we see what a person is to be and become, recognizing in Jesus Christ the paradigm of rightly ordered relationship with self, others, God, and the whole of creation.

In talk about the Trinity, a grammar that is sometimes stilted and foreign to our ears, we probe the truth that God speaks and breathes: in Word, in Spirit. God is not turned in; nor is God the Supreme Being in self-imposed, self-selecting, blissful isolation. God's very life is expressive, ecstatic, fecund. The category of relationality is central to all speech about the Trinity. The rules of grammar which form the Trinitarian doctrine are intended to help us see the profoundly relational character of God. Since "God is love," God's very being is to be in relation, that is, God's very life is the relationality and mutual self-gift that makes Love what it is. There never was, nor will be, a time or place when or where God is not Love loving.

In time and space Love becomes incarnate, human flesh, in the person of Christ, God's Word, God's self-expression. And Love is communicated in the Spirit, the gift of the very life, breath, of God dwelling within human hearts. The Word is Love itself, God's very life in human life, history, the church, the world. The Spirit is God's Breath at the heart of all the living. Those who hear the Word of truth and live with and by the Spirit of Love, recognizing the name of Jesus the Christ by the power of the Holy Spirit, cry out to the God beyond all names: "Father." Christian life in the Spirit, the Christian spiritual life, is a journey from and toward God, the one called "Father," who is the origin and end of Love. Christian life is living for God through Christ the Word, the truth irrevocably spoken: Life endures; Love endures. It is living with and in the Spirit dwelling in the depths of the human heart, living from the desire for fuller life, light, and love recognized in the self-giving of Jesus on the cross, the perfect image of interpersonal love.

To speak of God the Father, Son, and Spirit in the grammar of the Trinity is to say that God is not the solitude of a solitary essence, but the relational and personal mystery disclosed most fully in the event of the cross and Resurrection of Jesus the Christ. In his self-giving at the supper on the night before he died, and in his passion, death, and dying—unto death and into hell—Jesus speaks the very truth of the

Giver, Given, and Gift/ing which is Love itself. The Life that pours itself forth (Son) from, toward and for the originating Lover (Father) in and through Love (Spirit) is the very Love that endures. He who is Love itself, unto death and into hell, lives. Love lives. Love is loving—a gift still on offer.

It is God's creative, saving, and sanctifying acts in history, what God has done and is doing in history by the gift of the Son and Spirit, which is the starting point, or the principal focus, of all Christian life and practice, as well as of all theology. "God talk," speech about the Trinity, has all too often been understood as discourse about the intradivine life, the mystery within the Godhead. It is sometimes thought that theology's principal concern is God in Godself, untethered from what God the Father has done and is doing in Jesus through the presence and power of the Holy Spirit. It is little wonder, then, that the Trinity has been thought of as lofty, abstract, distant.

Further, the doctrine of the Trinity is often thought to be lofty and abstract because creation, redemption, and sanctification are conceived of as past events which took place in some long ago time, or time before time. But in learning to speak correctly of God through the grammar of the Trinity, we recognize more clearly that God is creating, saving, and sanctifying here and now, in our own time and place. God is Word express*ing* and Spirit animat*ing* here and now. God is speak*ing* and breath*ing*. Love is lov*ing*. A Trinitarian spirituality is a whole way of life by which we participate in the mission of Word and Spirit in human life, history, the church and the world, becoming ourselves expressions and configurations of God's speak*ing* and breath*ing*—now.

CHAPTER THREE

Bonded in the One Love: A Share in the Divine Life

T HE DOCTRINE OF THE TRINITY affirms the truth that God is Father, Son, Spirit—three in one Love—Giver, Given, Gift/ing. These three partake of the divine nature in distinct ways. Thus, we say that there are three persons in God. This God is personal, that is, Love's Pure Source is expressed in the Word and is active in the Spirit, bonding source and its expression. The relationality of the three bonded in the one Love spills over into a relationality with the world, thereby making it possible for human persons to enter into this communion in the one Love. The doctrine of the Trinity, a grammar of gift in which small words— the prepositions—play the key role, is intended to speak correctly of God the Father, Son, and Spirit, thereby deepening interpersonal communication and inviting participation in communion.

The grammar of the Trinity sets the parameters of speech about the mystery of God as Father, Son, and Spirit—three distinct divine persons. But the language of the three in one Love also opens up fresh horizons and future possibilities for understanding what it means to be a human person. For even as it speaks of the divine persons, the Trinitarian doctrine throws light on what Christians think a human person is. More specifically, the doctrine of the Trinity throws light on what kind of person a Christian is called to be and become through participation in the mission of Word and Spirit, thereby entering into communion in the one Love.

A governing concern in many approaches to spirituality today, inclusive of Christian spirituality, is the age-old question: Who am I? A Christian spirituality which is altogether Trinitarian poses the question quite differently: *Whose* am I? And this question is raised within the context of a more important question: What, or who, is God? It is only within this larger frame of reference that the question of personal identity may be settled. At least partially. For the human person, like Father, Son, and Spirit, distinct in relation to the other and to us, is mystery. What the grammar of the Trinity expresses is the conviction that relatedness is not external to the life of God, but constitutive of the divine life. Who and what we understand God to be is key in our effort to answer the question: Who am I? Naming God "Father, Son, Spirit," three in one Love, Trinity, is, then, not an abstraction. It articulates not only who and how we understand God to be, but what I am called to be and become. What, then, is this view of human persons that stems from the understanding of God as Father, Son, Spirit, three in distinct relations of interpersonal love?

Created in the image of God, Father, Son, and Spirit, personal identity—who, what, and how we are—is constituted by being in relationship. For human beings, personhood is not an always and already accomplished fact, but a gift received in the relations of interpersonal love. Human personhood is not something achieved in autonomy or independence or self-determination or self-sufficiency. Rather, human personhood is received in self-donation, being toward, always toward the other and others in relation. We come from others, we live with others. Our being is toward and for others. We come to ourselves only through and with others.

The doctrine of the Trinity conveys the truth that God is personal, *toward* and *for*—Love's Source expressed in Word and bonding in the Spirit, bonding source and expression. Saying that God is personal is to say that God is sheer loving relation in self-gift; that self-giving, mutuality, and interdependence are at the very heart of God's being God. The doctrine of the Trinity affirms that God is personal; God is not a by-itself, or an in-itself, or an in-and-of-itself, but rather God exists in a communion of persons toward one another in self-giving Love, revealed in Word and Spirit in human life, in history, in the world. God is immutably toward us and for us in the self-giving Love that is constitutive of the divine life. All reality is personal. Everything that exists is from God, in God, for God, who is God precisely in the relations of interpersonal self-giving Love: Father, Son, Spirit.

What are the implications of the Trinitarian grammar for our understanding of human beings, of human personhood? How do these insights into who God is and how God is throw light on basic human, and deeply spiritual, questions: Who am I? What am I to be? What kind of person do I want to become? How am I to live the one and only life I have to live?

Person: Toward and for the Other

The human person is not an individual, not a self-contained being who at some stage in life chooses or elects to be in relationship with another and others. From the very first moment of existence, the infant is toward the other, ordinarily the mother or father, who is in turn toward and for the infant. From our origin we are related to others. We are from others, by others, toward others, for others, just as it is in God to exist in the relations of interpersonal love. God is Love, three in the one Love: Father, Son, Spirit. God is Love in the relationality and mutuality constitutive of love. The grammar of the Trinity is the uniquely and specifically Christian way of speaking of the God who is not confined to a self-imposed and self-selecting heavenly solitary confinement. The Trinity is not some all-pervasive, ethereal, benign mist. God is Love. God is revealed as Love in Word and Spirit in the grand economy of redemption: The Father sends his only Son and gifts us with the Spirit in our hearts. Trinity is a way of speaking of a personal God who ex-ists—is out of and toward others in relation, who communicates, whom we come to know precisely as God for us, toward us, with us, in us. God is Love in the way that an emerald is green (Simone Weil), or a ruby red. And Love is life pouring itself forth. God is the Love that overspills, because Love cannot be contained. God is Love in excess, excessive of what reason might demand or justice require—gift.

At times Christian understandings of human personhood as well as of the spiritual life have been heavily influenced by

an understanding of the Trinity that emphasizes the three in
one Love mirrored in the inner life of the individual person.
In such a perspective, we come to a deeper knowledge of
God in an ever-deeper journey inward, wherein there are
vestiges of the Word, promptings of the Spirit of Love. God
is to be known in our own knowing and in our own loving.
But there is a danger that such a pursuit, if unchecked, may
result in self-preoccupation and self-absorption. A revitalized
understanding of the Trinity provides just such a check. For
it dispels distorted notions of the human person as a self-
sufficient individual and of God as the eternal solitary One.
Understanding God as Love, incarnate in Christ and communicated in the Spirit, that is, as Trinity, provides a critical
challenge to any understanding that sees either the human
being or God as self-contained individuals. God is self-giving
Love. And human destiny rests in receiving and living from
that gift in self-giving Love.

It is indeed correct that the human person is a unique
locus of God's self-disclosure and, given that we are created
in the image and likeness of God, it is natural to look for the
contours of that image within ourselves. However, the opening chapters of Genesis suggest that the image of God is to
be found in the relationship between persons. Male and fe-
male God created them. This gives the divine image in us a
dimension beyond the solitary self. Persons by definition
come into being through another, through others, and require others to exist. God is not first the eternal solitary One
who elects to be in relationship with the Son, thereby "becoming" personal. There never was a time or a place when or
where God was not Love. And Love pours life forth not into

a vacuum, but toward and for the other. God is the Love in the relationality that is constitutive of love. Love itself. It is the very nature of God to communicate Love, to Give, to be Given, to be Gift/ing. The being of God is to be the Giver of gift Given and Gift/ing, to express (Word) Love (Spirit).

Human personhood is both gift and task. We first experience ourselves as recipients of God's Gift/ing. The task of becoming an authentic human person involves accepting responsibility for our own growth to Christian maturity, recognizing our call to holiness through service in the church and the wider community. We embrace our call and accept our destiny by participating fully in the relations of interpersonal love, both human and divine, thereby being in communion with the living God, even here and now.

Such a view of human personhood and destiny is too often obscured in a culture wherein achievement, productivity, effectiveness, and usefulness have the upper hand. Looking to those persons we are inclined to overlook, to alternative ways of perceiving and being in the world, to "contrast experiences" (the term is Edward Schillebeeckx's), may throw light on who and what the human person is in Trinitarian perspective. Those who are wounded and weak, the last, littlest, and least in church and society, can be instructive in what it means to be human. They draw attention to forgotten and marginalized dimensions of ourselves. Indeed, those at the margins can be the teachers of the clever and the efficient. In particular, people with mental handicaps, the mentally retarded, the developmentally disabled, can open up new horizons of human personhood for the bright and the robust. This requires that we set aside tightly knit inherited

views of human nature as set in stone, an always already accomplished fact.

A note of caution is in order. The handicapped person
and others who are marginalized are not to be understood as
paradigms of human personhood. It is, rather, the three in
one Love, a relationality that spills over into the world, which
is the paradigm of human personhood. What is descriptive
and paradigmatic of human relationality is seen in Jesus
Christ, in the relationship of Son to Father, Father and Son in
the Spirit, and in Jesus' way of relating to all those he encoun-
tered. The handicapped are not models of all human personhood, but they can teach us something very important about
the gift and task of human personhood as participation in the
three in one Love. The handicapped, the wounded and the
weak, the last, the littlest, and the least often remind the
clever and the robust that the chief characteristic of the
human is to be open to relationship with others, to be constantly open to the Gift/ing which binds us together in a communion of Love. The human person has the capacity for this
from nature, but achieves it only by divine gift. That is, the
relationality which is openness to such love is realized in its
fullness only in a communion of Love, and only by divine gift.

Speaking Sheer Relation

By most standards, the mentally handicapped are not
equal to the smart and healthy, the "normal." The damage to
the brain or nervous system incurred during the pre-, peri-,
or post-natal period renders the mentally handicapped per-

son incapable of the normal exercise of intellect, deliberation, choice, and action. Perhaps the reason why the mentally handicapped are viewed as less than full persons is because they do not measure up to an abstract, given, a priori notion of what makes human beings human. If a particular view of human nature is judged as the measure of what constitutes personhood, then the mentally handicapped person's spontaneous shouts of glee or outbursts of rage and anger will appear as unnatural or, at least, not socially correct.

In the emergence of a Trinitarian grammar, the first consideration is given to the distinction and activity of the three who are God. The distinctiveness and uniqueness of the three is first. We begin by looking to Jesus Christ and the gift of the Spirit. Then emerges the question: How do they share in the divine nature, so that the divine character of redemptive and sanctifying work is assured? Following a Trinitarian logic, if person is first, then the uniqueness, the diversity, the great variety of distinct ones is where we need to begin in understanding the human. We do not begin with a fixed understanding of nature or essence or substance as something set in stone, something to which all are expected to measure up, in the face of which most fall short. Indeed, some are so wide of the mark that questions are raised as to whether they are human at all.

A Trinitarian spirituality rooted in an understanding of the three in the one Love attends to person as a distinct one, to distinct persons invited into communion in the one Love. The Father is originating Lover; the Son is the self-expression of Love; the Spirit is the inexhaustible self-giving of Love.

Rather than beginning with an abstract view of human nature, we begin by looking at the great range of distinct persons and speak about what human nature might be from that point of departure. What we see when we look to many mentally handicapped persons is that they are frequently, but not always, conspicuously relational with little pretense of self-sufficiency. They often must look toward the other, to others, for the fulfillment of basic human needs. But what we also see in many such persons are real qualities of heart, deep capacities for forgiveness, for reconciliation, for celebration, for mutuality, for tenderness, for compassion.

If person, specifically the mentally handicapped, is where we begin in seeking to understand the question of identity, we might see that what is unnatural to humans is all that does not enhance human, personal flourishing in the relations of interpersonal love expressed in forgiveness, reconciliation, reciprocity, compassion. It is such qualities that call forth the fullness of personhood, inviting and challenging us to be most fully human by being united in the one and same mutual Love. This is quite a different position from one in which persons are evaluated in view of their success or failure to achieve some fixed, a priori notion of human nature. If our point of departure in understanding human identity is with the great variety of distinct ones, the rich range of human persons and personalities, then a much wider understanding of human being and personal becoming is allowed in response to the call to ever deepening participation in the communion of persons, both human and divine.

Though vastly unequal to the bright and strong in terms of their capacities for intellectual growth and self-sufficiency,

the mentally handicapped are equal in dignity to them because all are created in the image of the three in one Love.
This equality is grounded in a personhood which derives from
the communion of divine persons, distinct and unique in their
relations. Each and every one, even those judged to be non-
human or sub-human or not-quite-human, is a person, that is,
toward the other, endowed with the capacity for relationship.
But the relationship may be of a wholly different order than
what is prized in a culture of conspicuous consumption, a society propelled by productivity and achievement.

The handicapped often remind us that our whole being
cries out for relationship. Often they have a heightened capacity and propensity for authentic communion. In the lives
of mentally handicapped persons there is very little hope or
chance of achieving or measuring up to some predetermined
notion of ideal human nature—what a man is supposed to be,
how a woman must act. The same is true for the seriously ill,
the comatose, the seriously injured, the aged, the dying.
Their personhood is not something achieved by brains and
brawn. It is gift.

In an age such as ours, which celebrates achievement and
productivity, the mentally handicapped are not successful.
They don't measure up. Handicapped persons don't really
produce or achieve very much with their hands. They seem
to have very little to contribute. But the mentally handicapped serve as catalyst in the recognition that one's personhood is not grounded in what one does or achieves. They remind all of us, highly intelligent, strong-willed overachievers,
that our basic humanity, who we are as persons, lies elsewhere. Moreover, the mentally handicapped person is often

unattractive physically and sexually, serving as a reminder that physical beauty and sexual allure do not constitute the person as person. The person is a being with a heart, one who has the capacity to be open to attraction by another, to be in communication and interpersonal communion with another, others, and God. This is what distinguishes us as persons: the capacity to be toward others in a relation of one, mutual Love. This deepest, most fundamental dimension of human personhood is all too often buried, suffocating beneath the veneer of physical beauty, easily sold out in the dynamics of sexual interchange. The handicapped help us to uncover forgotten dimensions in which the mystery of authentic human personhood rests.

The handicapped might serve to remind the clever and the strong that there is no strict equation between who we are as persons and our ability to think, to weigh, to decide, or to carry through with a specific course of action. The fullness of human personhood does not lie in our ability to think or to choose. Indeed, what makes the person a person is something prior to, deeper and more fundamental than intellect and will or thinking and choosing. It lies in the heart, in *affectus*, in the ability to be in relation, the relations of interpersonal love, in the capacity for self-giving as gift in response to divine gift. Intellect and will find their end in Love. In God. In a communion of persons in one Love.

Because they are often quite conspicuously relational, mentally handicapped persons remind us that human dignity and destiny are not to be found in unbridled autonomy. We are not autonomous. We do not name and shape our lives and destiny alone. And because their very existence is out of the mold, handicapped persons are not easily understood by others, not easily named by them, with the exception of the general label "handicapped." They serve as a reminder that our identity—"Who am I?"—is not settled by the way others name us, or call us, or label us. We are neither self-made selves nor defined by others; neither self-named, *autonomous*, nor named by others, *heteronomous*. We are named by God and find our identity in being from God, toward God, and for God: *Theonomous*. The human person is mystery, whose identity and destiny rest in the communion of persons, divine and human.

The *Theonomous* character of personhood is luminously disclosed in the lives of those who have very little to say in a world dominated by ideas and controlled by ideologies; little to decide in a world driven by the deep-seated need to manipulate and control; and very little to achieve in a world driven by lust for success, efficiency, and productivity. Indeed, we can learn something about what it means to be human persons precisely in and through those who, more often than not, are judged to be less than human persons.

The clever, the strong, and the robust can quite literally stand on their own two feet. The healthy and the strong are supposed to fend for themselves. But if the human person is a being toward the other, toward others, toward God, perhaps we can learn about this dimension of being toward from handicapped persons, as well as from others who are last, littlest, and least, those who invite us into relationship rooted in the one and same mutual Love, precisely because of their more obvious need of gift, of love.

The necessity of being in relationship to others is often denied by the clever, the strong, the robust, the healthy, even though we know in our marrow that it is an illusion to think that we are not ineluctably related. "Normal" people find countless ways to perpetuate the fantasy that relationship is external to who we are, and that there is a self-subsistent, self-made self that is prior to and somehow more real than the relations of interpersonal love that are constitutive of who we are. But to exist as a person is to be a distinct one in relation. Those with quite conspicuous needs serve as a smack-in-the-face reminder of this relational character which the clever and robust are all too often inclined to overlook or flatly deny.

In the handicapped person, and in others on the margins of society and church, we are confronted with the realization that our personhood is not based on intelligence, or on the ability to weigh and decide, or on the capacity to do or to achieve. Our personhood is both gift from God and response to God. We are not self-made selves. Because authentic personhood is rooted in God and not based on intelligence or on what we achieve, we are fundamentally equal one to another. Though we are different and distinct from one another, there is to be no subordination among us: woman to man, black to white, poor to rich, simple to smart, gay to straight. All are equal because human personhood is *Theonomous*: from God and for God. Therein lies our identity. Who we are is rooted in an understanding of God who is personal, in whom there is no subordination of one to another. The Son is not subordinate to Father, the Spirit is not subordinate to the Son. All share in the divine nature equally, though distinct in their relations.

In the grammar of the Trinity, the term *perichoresis* describes the active, mutual, equal relations between the Father, Son, and Spirit, without subordination. If the doctrine of the Trinity not only expresses what and who we think the divine persons are, but also articulates what human persons are called to be and become, then, in Trinitarian perspective, human beings are to cultivate, nurture, and sustain the kinds of relationships that are reflective of this *perichoresis*. In our dealings with one another there is to be always and everywhere a willingness to embody a spirit of equality and mutuality, true interdependence grounded in the equal dignity of each one. Even those who seem vastly unequal in terms of intelligence, productivity, or physical beauty have equal dignity as persons in light of the *Theonomous* character of human life.

If we are willing to set aside preoccupations and preconceptions of what makes human nature human, perhaps we can be open to the gift on offer in the lives of those who have very little to gain by social convention and virtually nothing to contribute in a world driven to succeed, those whose capacity for self-determination is severely and profoundly limited. By opening to them we may learn what it means to act in accord with our true nature, rather than according to social custom. Indeed, the mentally handicapped person may act more natural, more human, than the so-called "normal" person. It is far less natural, far less human, to exterminate millions of defenseless people than it is to shriek with joy or play the clown in public. Yet it was the "normal," the intelligent and efficient, those whose mental and volitional capacities were intact, who carried out the Final Solution during the Nazi regime. And it is the so-called "normal" who continue to devise more efficient programs of genocide. As survivors of the Holocaust and others are quick to point out, the methods of the Final Solution were implemented as if they were quite "normal," altogether justifiable because they were in service of a noble aim: the pure human specimen, the perfect human nature. This nobler aim, of course, required getting rid of those whose personhood was in doubt because of race, ethnicity, religion, physical impairment, sexual orientation.

What is judged "normal" may be a composite of layers of falsehood and illusions of self-sufficiency, the fantasies of the self-subsistent self. Mentally handicapped persons are incapable of harboring such illusions because their need for another and others and God at every level of their existence is so altogether conspicuous and irrefutable.

The mentally handicapped disclose what it means to be a person not by living some sustained, cherubic, cuddly existence, but by witnessing to the full range of human emotions, the deepest cries and joys of the human heart, without the defenses of false self, social correctness, or neighborly politesse. To be sure, authentic personhood is not synonymous with giving expression to any and all feelings, desires, and emotions. These are to be integrated within the task of personal becoming if true communion of persons is to be brought to fruition. But what is distinctive of many handicapped people, what marks them as different from the "normal," at least in part, is the immediacy of these experiences as well as their expression, negative as well as positive. The gift of many handicapped people is what appears to be a sort of constitutional inability to be other than what they are in all its immediacy—persons who are wide open for relationship,

for receiving a gift on offer. It is precisely in human brokenness and vulnerability that this openness to the gift of God's
giving, the *Theonomous* character of human personhood,
comes forth from beneath layers of political, religious, and
social correctness. Amidst the failure to measure up to a view
of human nature as an always already accomplished fact, we
come to recognize that who we are, or better, whose we are,
is gift.

Persons Human and Divine: In Communion

It is the call and destiny of each one of us to receive
God's gift of self-giving Love in Christ through the Spirit
and then to live with that gift and from it. Setting aside
tightly knit ideas of human nature against which individuals
are to be measured, we may look to all those who don't quite
measure up as disclosing horizons of an authentic communion of persons in mutuality, interdependence, equality. Each
one, distinct in relation to the others, is *Theonomous*: from
God, in God, for God.

Attentiveness to what can be learned from handicapped
persons should not obscure what is to be learned about personal identity from others who manifest in a particular way
the relationality which is the openness to union in the one
and same mutual Love. Sexual exchange, the perception and
pursuit of truth, beauty and justice, art, architecture, and
music are all expressions of a deep desire for communion,
giving form to the magnitude of God's love. They are to be
recognized as authentic ways of participation in the divine
life. Indeed, all authentic forms of interpersonal communica-

tion and communion are paths of deification. Of particular import in understanding a Trinitarian spirituality is a fuller appreciation of the sacramentality of marriage in which two are in relationship with one another in mutual self-giving, a giving which is bound and binding in love. In a giving which overspills into a wider and deeper inclusivity, the partners serve as an icon of Love's Breath in flesh, Jesus Christ.

Who we are as persons can be defined only in terms of our relation to God. We come from God and are toward God. Therein lies our name, our identity, who we are. Therein lies the answer to the question: "Who am I?" or "Whose am I?" And this is true of all creation, not just of human beings, but of non-human life as well: everything that exists is from God and finds its destiny in giving praise and glory to God. All that exists participates in personal existence through the creative activity of God. Everything that exists is relational insofar as it comes from God and is for God's praise and glory—even grasshoppers, llamas, palm trees! Non-human life does not exist except in and through God who is altogether personal, relational through and through.

This view is consistent with traditional views in which it is understood that all of creation exists to greater or lesser degree in the life of God. Every living thing participates in some measure in God's being. Now, if God is understood as personal, as being *toward* and *for*, then every living thing is toward and for the other, existing to varying degrees in communion with the God whose providential plan is not just for the salvation of the human race, but for the salvation of the whole world. Everything that is reaches its destiny by existing toward and for the praise of God's glory.

Such a view is also in accord with the emergent awareness and appreciation of the relational character of all reality, of the whole cosmos, of the interconnectedness inherent to everything in the universe. It is not just the human person who is created in the image of God. All creation bears vestiges, traces of the living God, a profoundly relational mystery.

As this God is God for us in the economy of salvation, so the human person exists by being ever more fully toward and for others through continually deepening participation in communion of persons, human and divine. The *telos* or end of human personhood is received as a gift in the encounter with all those who invite us into a fuller participation in the one and mutual Love, a relationality within which is disclosed what it means to be human in its fullness by divine gift. This is our destiny. In this lies deification: to receive all as gift and thereby to find and give the gift of self in the communion of interpersonal love, both human and divine.

At the end of the day, it is not our achievements, our doing, that will count the most. Rather, true brilliance is the glory of God transforming each and all of us into sons and daughters of the Father through Christ in the Spirit, bonding all together in a communion in the one Love. Transformed by the very light and life of God, this is what we become: a blessed communion of persons both human and divine.

Those who have very little in the way of worldly goods, or in the ways of the wisdom of this earth, invite us to this way of perceiving and being. So, too, do all those who open up the human heart to the superabundance of Love's loving in our own time and place, inviting us into communion with the three in one Love, embracing diminishment and anguish,

relishing the gift yet to be given even in dying and death. For
even and especially in our brokenness and failure, when there
is nothing left but loss, and yet more loss, the glory of God
shines: alight in the face and piercing eyes of the one who
faced diminishment, darkness and death—the Son of the Father, perfect icon of Love, Given and Gift/ing.

The doctrine of the Trinity speaks not only of the three
in one Love, but expresses what the Christian person is called
to be and become. In understanding the human, attention
must be given not only to what is had in common, but also to
what is distinct. Indeed, this is where we must begin in coming to a fuller understanding of the human. It is the distinction and activity of the three who are one God in the economy of salvation which was and remains central in answering
theology's single most important question: Who is God?
From the perspective of a Trinitarian spirituality, the question "Who am I?" is answered only through participation in
the mission of Word and Spirit by which the world is transformed by and in the one Love.

CHAPTER FOUR

Speaking in a Fleshly Way: Participation in the Mission of Word and Spirit

W E BEGIN TO REFLECT on the mystery of who God is through the Son given and in the gift/ing of the Spirit. Through the Son and in the Spirit we are drawn into relationship with the Father. To be Christian is to be caught up in the relationship between Father and Son in the Gift of Love bonding Love and its expression, even now. But we are able to participate in the life of the three in one Love only because it has been made manifest in the Word made flesh by the power of the Holy Spirit.

By the Incarnation of the Word, God enters human life, history, the world. But the Incarnation also makes it possible for us to enter the very life of God. Through the Incarnation, God became part of our eating and drinking, our sickness, our joy, our delight, our passion, our dying, our death. But all this is for the purpose of drawing us out of ourselves, away from our own self-preoccupation, self-absorption, self-fixation, so as to participate in the divine life.

Sunday by Sunday, Christians all over the world come together for the celebration of the Eucharist. After hearing the word of God proclaimed in scripture, and before approaching the table of the Lord, we profess our faith in the words of the Creed. We affirm that by the power of the Spirit, God's Word took flesh of the Virgin of Nazareth. This is for us, and for our salvation. God in human flesh is at the center of Christian faith. What we celebrate Sunday by Sunday rests on the Father's gift of the Son, God's Word in human flesh through the gift of the Spirit. All else that the Christian might affirm about God, whatever the grammar of the Trinity might seek to express, depends upon God's Word becoming flesh, the consummate expression of the Father's love, which we can recognize because of the gift of the Holy Spirit, Love itself, given to us and giving. When we give thanks for the creative, saving, and sanctifying acts of God the Father, the Son, and the Spirit, we can do this precisely because the Word became flesh by the power of the Spirit and made a dwelling with us (Jn 1:14).

Believing in the Incarnation entails more than affirming a truth about God. It is beholding the glory of God in the person of Jesus Christ, the perfect icon of the Father, perfect in self-giving love. But this can be done only by the prompting of the Spirit's gift dwelling within the human heart. Saying yes to the mystery of the Incarnation is the Spirit-assisted response by which we embrace a whole way of life for the Father's glory through Christ in the Spirit. It means living as brothers and sisters to Christ, children of the Father, in a filial spirit of trust and hope-filled confidence rooted in the utter reliability of God's gift given in the Incarnation of Love itself (Jn 1:12).

Through the Incarnation of God's Word in Jesus Christ, the gift of God's love, God's very life itself, is immutably turned toward us creatures with whom God has freely and irrevocably entered into covenant. God speaks and acts preeminently in and through the humanity of Jesus Christ. This union of the divine and human in Jesus Christ is designated the "hypostatic union," expressing the conviction that the humanity of Jesus is ineluctably united in the person, the *hypostasis*, of the Word, the second person of the Trinity—God for us and toward us in Christ. Jesus the Christ is God's Word, God's self-expression, God's speech, God's act, God's own deed in human life, history, the world. He is God among us, known in the presence and power of the Spirit, God's own Breath.

God comes to us in the embrace of human flesh. While "flesh" here is understood to mean that "God has skin," it also means that God takes on the whole of human life and history, indeed all creation. "Becoming flesh" refers not only to the conception and birth of Jesus from the flesh of Mary, but also to the embrace of the human condition in its entirety in the whole life and ministry, passion, dying, death, and raising of Christ to new life. In the Incarnation, God enters into a glorious exchange with humanity, an exchange which is always at God's gracious initiative, and in which God is Giver, Given, and Gift/ing. The Gift and Giving is God's presence to the human reality, in its joys and delights as well as in its woundedness and fragility. Linked with the mystery of Incarnation is the *kenosis*, the self-emptying of God's own life into human life, history, the church, and the world. Through the cross, Christ is emptied in death and into hell, for Love itself knows no bounds. This divine self-emptying is celebrated in the great hymn in Saint Paul's Letter to the Philippians, where, in reference to Jesus Christ, Paul exclaims: "Though he was in the form of God, he did not regard equality with God as something to be exploited, but he emptied himself, taking the form of a slave, being born in human likeness. And being found in human form, he humbled himself, and became obedient to the point of death—even death on a cross!" (Phil 2:6-8).

Too often, in the face of this central Christian mystery, we are inclined to stop and adore. But nowhere in the gospels does Jesus urge us to adore him. Rather, he asks us to follow him, the one sent. And by following him and being sent together with him, we participate in his life, his energy, the Spirit, the Breath of God. This is to live the divine life—even now.

Love Speaking and Breathing

By the mystery of the Incarnation, God's love is made manifest, present to the human reality. He is light amidst darkness, the divine life amidst human life, recognized as God's manifestation by the wise ones who followed his star (Mt 2:1-12). He is God's Word in flesh. The Father speaks a Word, and his name is Jesus Christ, the Son. Here "Word" does not mean just an instrument of verbal communication. Word is expressivity, speech. Here it is God's speech. But speaking is not possible without breath. Indeed, speaking and breathing are inherently related. In Word and Spirit, God is speaking and breathing the divine life in the world.

Self-expression, speech, takes many different forms. We each express ourselves in ways well beyond the verbs and nouns we use. We speak through body language, gesture, our clothing and the rings we wear. We speak through the glance of an eye that comforts or condemns, through dance, ritual, celebration, touch, kiss, sexual intimacy. We speak in action. Throughout our lives, from infancy through old age, we are "speechifying," expressing.

God, too, communicates, "speechifies," expresses, most directly in Jesus the Christ, the Word of God incarnate, God in flesh. What is being said? What is being expressed? What is being seen in speech made visible in a fleshly way? We need only cast a glance at the gospels.

In and through the Word, God feeds, weeps, and washes. Jesus the Christ is silent and listens because he wants to learn. He works just like most everyone else in Nazareth, and grows from childhood through adolescence to adulthood. He celebrates, and probably enjoys the good wine at Cana. He visits. He goes to the home of Simon Peter, and there enjoys being served a good meal. He eats and rests. He craves quiet, prays and sleeps. He feels pain. He touches, touches even sin. He heals, he suffers, and he dies.

A Christian spirituality which is Trinitarian through and through looks to Jesus Christ the Incarnate Word of God, attentive to the gift/ing of the Holy Spirit dwelling in our deepmost self, in the heart. It entails the discipline of receiving the gift of the Father through the Word in the Spirit. But the gift of God, God's presence in human life, is given amidst the glory and the fragility of the human reality. Within the context of earthly reality we receive the creative, saving, sanctifying acts of Father, Son, and Spirit amidst the humdrum of our often very ordinary lives, lives given to simple acts such as feeding and washing and working. God is with us in our listening, in the sometimes deadening but often consoling silence. The divine presence is to be discerned while we travel, as we teach and learn. God's nearness is to be known in our weeping and in our walking, as we move alongside others through the various stages of life's journey. When we visit the sick, the elderly and the infirm, as he did, God is in our midst. And God is there at our table when we invoke Christ's name and enjoy the fruits of the earth. There, too, in the pain, in the darkness, in the hurt, in the loss, in our very brokenness and vulnerability. God is seen in the healing gaze, touched in the hand that comforts, heard in the word that encourages, and welcomed in offering ourselves as a gift.

A Trinitarian spirituality rooted in the Incarnate Word of God who is the perfect image of the Father is a way of perceiving and being seized and saturated by the gift of God's love amidst the mundane, the ordinary, the routine. It is a way of life rooted in the recognition that all is gift to be received. And it is to live freely with, in, and from that gift.

Trinitarian spirituality is nothing more, or less, than a baptismal spirituality. In baptism we are conformed to Christ, anointed with the Spirit, gifted by the Father to live as sons and daughters of God, brothers and sisters in Christ. Through baptism we are invited to participate in the mission of Word and Spirit. This mission, brought to its fullness in the cross and Resurrection of Love incarnate, is clearly made manifest in the baptism of Jesus in the Jordan by John.

> And when Jesus had been baptized, just as he came up from the water, suddenly the heavens were opened to him and he saw the Spirit of God descending like a dove and alighting on him. And a voice from heaven said, "This is my Son, the Beloved, with whom I am well pleased."
> Then Jesus was led by the Spirit into the wilderness to be tempted by the devil. (Mt 3:16–4:1)

Through Christian baptism, we participate in the life and mission of Word and Spirit. This mission is made manifest in the theophany at the river. Jesus is named "Son" by the Father in the Spirit. But in this very naming, the Son is the one sent, impelled by the Spirit to be tempted by the devil and to combat evil. He preaches the reign of God, announces the good news that in the time of God's favor the oppressed are set free, the blind see. Indeed, in his words and in his work, Jesus embodies God's intention for the world now and to come, a world transfigured in and by Love. Jesus' life was not a free and easy ride, but a continual struggle against injustice and hate, illness, suffering, and depersonalization. The reign of God, God's intention for the world now and to come, is realized only in a communion in the one Love, which Jesus manifests most fully at the table on the night before he dies and in his self-giving on the cross, anticipated in his Transfiguration on Mount Tabor (Mt 17:1-8; Mk 9:2-8; Lk 9:28-36; 2 Pet 1:16-18).

Word and Spirit are made manifest, thereby inviting our active participation in the mission through which the world is transformed by Love itself into a communion in the one Love. At once sent forth and carried by the mission of Word and Spirit, it is our gift and task to participate in Love's expressive and creative animating activity in the world. Who we are as persons is realized in bringing forth Love and in all creative expressions of the one Love. It is ours to live in the flow of life in and from the mission of Christ and Spirit— moving into deeper communion with the three in one Love.

Word is Love heard and seen. Spirit is the principle of Love's creativity and bonding. In the Son and the Holy Spirit, God is speaking and breathing. Word is what is said, Spirit is the saying. What is said in the saying is Love. But Love expressed and bonding takes many different forms. To participate in the mission of Word and Spirit is to see and to share in the manifold manifestations of human expressivity and creativity as they disclose the divine reality. The Christian call is to flow with and in the missions of Word as expressivity and Spirit as creativity, communicating and bringing forth the one Love. In human expressivity and in various configurations of human creativity and bonding we come to know something of the magnitude of the God who is three in one Love. Our gift and task is to cultivate, to nurture and sustain the great variety of the manifestations of the magnitude of God's love in all forms of expressivity and creativity. Human life and destiny are ultimately realized not in the exercise of individual rights and liberties, but in all those creative expressions of Love that lead to a fuller communion in the one Love.

Beholding Together the One Love

We need only look at the expressivity of the artist, the poet, the musician, the gardener, the dancer, the architect—indeed, of all who are engaged in creative endeavor. They bring together a wide range of elements—textures, colors, sounds, movements—into the creative act, inviting us to a realization of the magnitude of Love. Precisely through their expression and creativity they bring us to a fuller taste of communion.

The depth of the human desire for expressivity and creativity is seen in the testament left to us by Jean-Dominique Bauby in *The Diving Bell and the Butterfly*. On December 8, 1995, the forty-three-year-old Bauby, who was editor-in-chief of the French fashion magazine *Elle* and the father of two young children, suffered a massive stroke. The paralysis was complete, with the exception of the ability to blink his left eye. Like a deep sea explorer going down in the water encased in an iron bell, Bauby was now locked in his own body, unable to move or to speak—except with his left eye.

Gradually, in the course of suffering "locked-in syndrome," Bauby learned to indicate letters of the alphabet by blinking his eye. Since "e" is the letter used with greatest frequency in French, one blink signaled the letter "e." "A" was signaled with a certain number of blinks; the least commonly used letters were signaled with the largest number of blinks. Thus, each letter of the alphabet could be indicated by a certain number of blinks. Letters could be strung together into words by blinking the left eye. These became the blocks for sentences which in turn flowed into paragraphs, then into the chapters which form the book *The Diving Bell and the Butterfly*.

The spirit soars with the blink of an eye. The paralysis is complete, but it cannot extinguish Bauby's desire to express himself, to tell what he sees day in and day out, to narrate the beauty he sees, through one eye, in the gathering of clouds over the coast at Berck-sur-Mer, the seaside town where he is terminally "locked-in" to a hospital for invalids. He speaks of things from his past, of tastes and smells and sights, fresh in the mind's eye, and of loss. Profound loss. Blinking, he reaches out to express his love for his daughter Céleste and his son Théophile—just children, now deprived of the touch of a father's embrace. Hunched in his wheelchair, he plays a game of hangman with Théophile by blinking out his moves:

> I guess a letter, then another, then stumble on a third. My heart is not in the game. Grief surges over me. His face not two feet from mine, my son Théophile sits patiently waiting—and I, his father, have lost the simple right to ruffle his bristly hair, clasp his downy neck, hug his small, lithe, warm body tight against mine. There are no words to express it. My condition is monstrous, iniquitous, revolting, horrible. Suddenly I can take no more. Tears well and my throat emits a hoarse rattle that startles Théophile. Don't be scared, little man, I love you.

He longs for the fullness of life and of love, expressing his desire for that fullness, creating and animating a loving communion with his children, into which we and countless others are invited to participate—with the blink of an eye.

In 1996 Jean-Dominique Bauby established the Association of Locked-In Syndrome. He died on March 9, 1997.

Traces of the magnitude of the one Love shimmer in the architecture of the new Getty Center in Los Angeles. The building combines classical forms with a postmodern feel for the random and near chaotic. Old and new are joined. At first glance, it may not seem to cohere; it does not seem to work as architecture. Some are startled by the first sight of it from a distance: "What *is* that?" But the architecture can be appreciated only within the space itself. On its mountain perch in Los Angeles, the structure's sharp, flat, glimmering surface contrasts with the warm, textured Travertine marble. Balconies provide layered spaces for human figures who scan the horizon for a glimpse of Westwood, Hollywood, downtown Los Angeles to the east and the mountains rolling toward the massive Pacific to the west. Looking south, the eye catches the long stream of cars traveling north and south on the San Diego Freeway. Gardens for strolling, laced by a flowing stream, are kissed by the southern California sunshine most days of the year. Fountains, promenades, cafés all contribute to the sense that this is indeed one of the world's most inviting public spaces. Strangely, many of the visitors to the Getty Center never manage to visit its museums. Precisely the point! So taken by the space, by the interplay of textures, by the nuance of color, by the interaction of light and surface, sea and sky, creamy marble and dozens of shades of purple flowers, visitors just linger and loll in the various parts of this place. For this is, above all, a people's place. Magnificent as the design may be, it is, as it were, a simple setting for a jewel. And the jewel is the human person, humanity in all diversity and uniqueness—coming together here, perching on balconies, ascending and descending staircases, moving together alongside others through the gardens, holding a child's hand, sipping a cool drink in an open-air café, looking, gazing, beholding, longing and, above all, being transfixed by the beauty of very earthly realities which, through the artistic act, allow an unspeakable mystery to stand forth. In this one place, we catch a glimpse of the range of creation, we touch its many textures, smell a plethora of aromas, and marvel at the diversity of earthly reality, and especially of human beings. Here we are invited to behold the magnitude of God's love which at once gives rise to such breath-stopping diversity while gathering it in and holding it all together.

There is a small and newly founded community of Trappistine nuns in Ecuador, a country rich in culture, natural beauty, and earthly resources. Its people are desperately poor; their national currency has been devalued to such a point that it is virtually worthless. The nuns' monastery is in Esmeraldas near the Pacific, in the coastal lowlands to the west of the Andes. It was at Esmeraldas that the Spanish first entered Ecuador. The climate is tropical. The geography can be described only as jungle-like. The monastery itself is a gem. Simple, stark, and spare, it is, nonetheless, a precious gem.

The community includes women of the indigenous peoples, *indígenas*, very dark of skin, who come from the high Sierra of the Andean range. There are also several sisters from Spain who left their home monastery to start the monastic foundation of Nuestra Señora de la Esperanza in Esmeraldas. Then there are the *mestizas*, those who are of mixed blood—Spanish and indigenous. And then there are some black Ecuadorian sisters who come from the western lowlands near Esmeraldas.

The nuns gather seven times a day for common prayer. They begin with Vigils long before dawn; they end with Compline just as the sun begins to set. They follow the well-worn tradition of simple psalmody as the mainstay of their life of prayer. At Esperanza in Esmeraldas, the rhythm of prayer is much like that of other Trappist and Trappistine monasteries throughout the world: patterned, predictable, repeatable. But for great liturgical feasts or other occasions of celebration, the rhythm of prayer is enlivened by *el ritmo*, the palpable rhythm coursing through the veins of the Ecuadorian sisters. Bodies sway in the choir stalls, hands are raised in clapping, voices ring out in jubilant song as two or three of the nuns, now dressed in glistening, flowing, floor-length garments and headdresses of coral and turquoise instead of the white and black Trappist habit and veil, dance and sway with flowers and pots of incense from the back of the church to its front, inviting all present to be taken up into *el ritmo* of drum, pan flute, tambourine, and marimba. At such celebrations one finds oneself in the flow of a creative and bonding energy that draws one into communion with these women of prayer—brown, black, and white—and, together with them, into fuller union in the one Love which gathers and keeps them together in mutual love and service.

God who is Love expresses that Love in a fleshly way in and through energy/breath in a creative and ongoing way.

The gift, the task, is to attend to the manifold manifestations of Word and Spirit in all human expressivity and creativity which invites participation in the one Love. But for the Christian, these must always be referred back to the Word in flesh, Jesus Christ, and to his Pasch.

Church: Love's Body Breathing

The mission of Word and Spirit—expressing, communicating, bringing forth a communion in the one Love—is expressly taken up in and by the church. As we live with and in this mission, and as we are carried in the flow of it, the church itself becomes a theophany. Christ is the worldly form of the action of the Spirit. In Christ, God speaks and breathes. But Christ empties himself, not only in the Incarnation, but also on the cross, and is now incarnate through the Breath of God animating the Body, the church. The manifestation of Christ continues to show forth in the church and its various activities which constitute its mission of being and building a communion in the one Love. Though the manifestations of the abundance of God's love are to be seen in all human expressivity, creativity, and bonding, it is particularly in the church, the Body of love in flesh and breath, that the presencing of Word and Spirit in the world over against the reign of Satan is to be found.

Understandings of the church have been marked by the historical and theological development of the doctrine of the Trinity. In some understandings of the church the prominence has been given to Christ, often to such an extent that the importance of the Holy Spirit has been eclipsed. The

Spirit has often become something like the proverbial middle child, inadvertently neglected and overshadowed because of the attention given to the others. This has had the lamentable effect of subordinating the Spirit to Christ, if not in theory, then inarguably in practice.

Some traditional definitions of the church rest on the conviction that its foundation lies in the person of Jesus Christ and in the mission entrusted to the Twelve. In this view, Christ himself established the church and entrusted its keys to Peter. The bestowal of the Spirit at Pentecost, on the other hand, signaled the birth of the church, but even more so, it marked the beginning of the mission to preach the good news to all the ends of the earth. A considerable amount of reflection on the nature of the church has been focused on the role of Christ in the church, particularly in its institutional structure. The church's mission in and to the world has been understood largely in terms of the pneumatic or charismatic, the presence and action of the Spirit. It is then an easy theological move to assert that the successors of the Twelve have a mission that comes directly from Christ. The bishops and those who through ordination share in their ministry, along with those who have an explicit ecclesiastical affiliation through religious vows, are entrusted to care for the life of the church. All the others, the laity, share in the mission of the Spirit given in baptism and confirmation. Their mission is to live the gospel in the world, that is, beyond the church, being and becoming a sanctifying, transforming presence in the midst of a world often envisioned as depraved, debauched, decadent, and altogether hostile to the gospel.

The problem with this conception of the church-world relationship is that it rests on a very unsatisfactory understanding of the equality, mutuality, and interdependence of Christ and Spirit. It is precisely in and through the Spirit that Christ established the church as a community of discipleship. When Christians preach, teach, heal, and live lives of mercy and compassion, they do this in the presence and by the power of the Spirit. Envisioning the church-world relationship in terms of sacred and secular, institution and charism, christic and pneumatic, ministry within the church and ministry in the world rests on a bifurcation, a rupture of Christ and Spirit that finds little justification in a proper understanding of the Trinity. The *perichoresis* descriptive of the equality, mutuality, and interdependence of the divine life of Father, Son, and Spirit also describes how they exist within the church itself as missioned in and to the world. The Body of Christ, the church, is built up in and through the Spirit, so it can act in the world in the Spirit.

This is appropriately expressed in the Second Vatican Council's image of the church as sacrament *in* and *to* the world. Christian spirituality rooted in a fresh understanding of the Trinity rejects the subordination of Spirit to Christ, world to church, lay to ordained and religious, secular to sacred. A vast array of Christian life-forms emerge in response to the Spirit who enlightens, enlivens, guides, sanctifies, and heals. The Holy Spirit is the Spirit of God, the Spirit of Christ in human life, history, and all creation. There can be no denying the Spirit's presence outside the church, in all forms of Love's speaking and breathing, in Love made flesh in the manifold human configurations of love.

Continuing Incarnation

The Word is speaking, the Spirit breathing. Jesus is *still* saying. We do not yet know who he is fully. The doctrine of the Resurrection of Jesus Christ communicates the truth that Christ now lives in the church in all its members. But it is especially in the church's sacramental life that the Incarnation continues. The sacramental life of the church constitutes the ritual core of communion in the one Love, the heart and soul of our participation in the life of the three in one Love.

From such a perspective, the sacramental life of the church may be seen as a way of "speechifying" our response to gift, expressing our thanks for the gift of God's constant giving. But in speaking our thanks we depend on those very earthly realities that are embraced in the Incarnation of the Word and enlivened by the Spirit of God: bread and wine, water and oil.

Sacrament is the language of God's constant coming, continual giving. In the sacramental life of the church, the Incarnation continues. It is in the sacraments that we receive and celebrate God's ongoing gift amidst the moments and seasons of human life. We do so with the simplest of elements, with earthly gestures, by means of very human and humanizing actions.

In baptism, we bathe, wash, cleanse. We purify with cool water. We strip naked and clothe in simplest white, letting the candle's light catch the eye and illumine the mind.

In confirmation there is the hand's touch, a word of encouragement and commitment, sending forth to do good things, oil to seal and replenish, and talk of tongues of fire that loosen lips to speak strong words of justice and mercy.

At the eucharistic table, we gather and greet, welcome and listen and speak. There is admonishing, asking, bringing gifts, blessing, singing, thanking, breaking bread, pouring wine, eating and drinking from a common plate and cup. And going forth.

In the sacrament of penance there is speaking and listening, whispering and weeping, consoling, pardoning, and receiving forgiveness. There is the desire to live from a grateful heart, and the hope of beginning again. And again.

The sacrament of anointing and pastoral care of the sick and dying soothes with oil, offers the healing that comes with touch, the chance to gather with family and friends to give and receive comfort. And words to encourage, give strength for the struggle, hope amidst the darkness of trial.

In celebrating Christian marriage there are words of fidelity, a pledge of self-sacrificial love, laying down of bodies, the nitty-gritty of sexual passion and the delight of its pleasure—blessed by God for life, the life of the whole world.

In the sacrament of holy orders there is a laying on of hands, an anointing with oil, the passing of a book, a commitment to service and self-sacrifice, and the promise of a single-hearted love that sets aside other loves—for Christ in the Spirit.

In much the same way that the doctrine of the Trinity can obscure the mystery of God's unbounded love rather than make it plain, so too can sacramental language and sacramental theology deafen us to the utterance of God's giving in sacrament. The language of priestly power or community action, or the rhetoric of what is changed in sacrament, or what the sacrament does for us, may muffle our hearing God's "speechifying" in the gift given, received, and celebrated. For sacrament, too, is first and finally gift through and through. It is gift received and celebrated. Our first response is not to give back, return, pay back, but to receive the gift again and again amidst earthly reality, to celebrate that presence through the Word in the Spirit to the glory of God the Father—and then to live freely and responsibly from the gift in the presence of the divine. Living freely with, in, and from the gift entails a deep recognition that all is gift, that the nature of sin lies in squandering the gift, and that responding to God's gift calls for living as stewards of all creation, as guests in God's household.

In Christ, all is embraced. He was not ashamed to call us brothers and sisters (Heb 2:11-13). Our life, every inch and ounce of it, every moment of it, is to be lived in the presence of the divine. In the tub and at the table. In our resting and our rising. In childbearing and child rearing. In sickness. In listening. In learning. In stripping and in clothing. In primping and in perfuming. In traveling. In the delight of sexual intimacy. But especially in our brokenness and in our vulnerability. All these ordinary and quite mundane human realities are paths to communion in the one Love. In artistic expression and in the sacramental life of the church we see more clearly the whole of the human reality as a precinct of epiphany, the geography of grace, the region of God's constant coming as gift.

Deifying Flesh

The mission of the church is to be a theophany, a light to
the nations, by being and becoming a manifestation of the
ongoing expression and creativity of Word and Spirit. This
we do as we struggle to learn to speak of and to God correctly and truthfully, even as we recognize the limits of all
speech about God. The theophanous character of the church
stands forth in sacrament and worship through which the
beauty of God is brought forth in simple gifts and in human
hearts transfigured by word and sacrament. Perhaps above all
else the church is a theophany when its members strive to
create a world in which all may grow, particularly those who
are wounded and weak, the last, the littlest, and the least,
those who are able to lead us to the heart of the communion
in one Love, those in whose broken bodies, as in the body of
Crucified Love, we can recognize deified flesh.

> Jesus took with him Peter and James and his brother
> John and led them up a high mountain, by them-
> selves. And he was transfigured before them, and his
> face shone like the sun, and his clothes became daz-
> zling white. Suddenly there appeared to them Moses
> and Elijah talking with him. Then Peter said to
> Jesus, "Lord, it is good for us to be here; if you wish,
> I will make three dwellings here, one for you, one for
> Moses, and one for Elijah." While he was still speak-
> ing, suddenly a bright cloud overshadowed them,
> and from the cloud a voice said, "This is my Son, the
> Beloved; with him I am well pleased; listen to him!"

> When the disciples heard this, they fell to the ground
> and were overcome by fear. But Jesus came and
> touched them, saying, "Get up and do not be afraid."
> And when they looked up they saw no one except
> Jesus himself alone. (Mt 17:1-8)

In the accounts of the Transfiguration of Jesus on Mount Tabor, a voice first heard at the Jordan is heard again: "This is my Son." The mission made manifest in his baptism will be brought to completion in the self-gift at the table and on the cross as the manifestation of the superabundance of God's love. He moves from manifestation through mission to manifestation, and from water to table to cross. So we are transfigured and become a theophany, growing in grace from font to table to cross. It is a way of deified flesh. But this never happens in isolation. At the Transfiguration on Tabor, Jesus is flanked by Moses and Elijah, embodiments of an ancient tradition of law and prophecy, and he is in the presence of the living: Peter, James, John. The transfiguration of human flesh becoming theophany occurs in relation to all the living and the dead, to the Father whose voice is heard at the Jordan and on Tabor, as well as to those who are yet to come. The anticipation of what is yet to come is signaled by each of the synoptic writers who introduce the story of the Transfiguration with Jesus' call to take up his cross and follow him. Light and glory are ineluctably related to pain and suffering. The Transfiguration is a theophany of hope in the face of loss and abandonment.

This is best expressed by the noticeable absence of explicit reference to the Holy Spirit in the accounts of the Transfiguration. Perhaps the Holy Spirit's presence and action are represented by the enfolding cloud, or expressed in the touch which casts out fear. But it is rather more that the Holy Spirit is the Gift/ing of God anticipated and anticipating, longed for and longing, hoped for and hoping. This Gift/ing in its fullness is given only in the cross and Resurrection anticipated in the Transfiguration. In anticipation, longing, and hope, we are drawn into and carried by the relationship between Father and Son through the cross and Resurrection to the fullness of Gift/ing at Pentecost when the Gift/ing brings to form the Body of Christ, the church carrying forward the mission of Word and Spirit.

The dazzling on Tabor is momentary. The vision of Jesus' deified flesh discloses to the disciples not only the glory of God, but also what it means to be most fully human. Beholding Jesus transfigured, the disciples are staggered. They see not only Jesus, but themselves. On Mount Tabor they are given a new vision, not only of Jesus the Christ, but of what the human person is to be and become: deified flesh.

The sudden blinding light of divine refulgence passes quickly. The disciples long to put up tents, to stay with, linger with, the dazzling of the light. But the gift, the task, is not to linger but—now freed from fear—to leave Mount Tabor with their faces toward Jerusalem, to go back into the city, the mundane, the ordinary, the routine, and therein to be open to all new manifestations of Love.

The theophany of deified flesh appears within the humdrum of the everyday, even and especially as we are taken up with seemingly countless demands, the never-ending exigencies of human life in a complex world. But learning how to see the glory of God amidst the harshness and the grandeur of the human reality takes discipline, an asceticism of looking, an *ascesis* of receptivity to all creative expressions of Word and Spirit, drawing us into communion in the one Love.

The light of Tabor enlightens the mind and heart to recognize that moments of luminosity are to lead back to a fuller sense of responsibility in ordinary life. More important, they are to draw us to the activity of justice, creating a world in which all may grow, seeing in each and every one, but especially in the last, the littlest, and the least, an invitation to share in the communion in one Love by which we, as persons and communities, are deified.

The image of Tabor expresses the truth that light is at the center of the experience of Christian prayer, contemplation, mysticism. One goes up the mountain by the path of *ascesis*—participating in the mission of Word and Spirit. In our day we have no direct access to the glory of God shining on Mount Tabor. We go up the mountain by rejecting and being rejected by the world, identifying with those who are most broken, those in whose vulnerability and brokenness we glimpse the shimmering crucified flesh of Christ. This is how we encounter the divine splendor in our own time and place.

Experiences of seeing and tasting and resting in the spiritual life are often quite fleeting. In the all-too-brief moments of theophany we are urged to move on from the moment and, delivered from all fear, to take up again the concrete concerns of building—through the demands of the humdrum and the ordinary, as well as by social and political action—a world in which all may grow.

Tabor's light shines in the experience of human brokenness and loss, and in the deep desire for communion in the one Love. God's grandeur is seen in the self-giving of Christ at the table and on the cross, pouring Word and Spirit into his new Body, the church itself. The church, then is gift/ed to be and become a theophany of love in flesh and breath, the house of Tabor's light for all the nations. This it does in its prayer, as Christians dare to call upon God as Father, through the Son, in the Spirit, to worship God in spirit and in truth, and to build a world in which all might live and grow as an act of praise to the glory of God.

The brilliance dazzles. Transfigured in the glory of God, Jesus is the perfect icon of the Father's unbounded love. In the Transfiguration we see what a person is called to be: transformed into sheer relation through self-gift, even unto death. On Tabor, the voice of God is heard once again: "This is my Son, the Beloved; with him I am well pleased." But even as Jesus is shot through with the love and light of the Father, Love's gift is yet to be fully given in the darkness of the agony, passion, and death of the Father's Son on the cross. It is there that God's glory is fully revealed in the complete self-gift of the Son, the consummate act of love which alone makes Love believable. Love given through life.

CHAPTER FIVE

Living Freely from the Gift:
The Grammar of Spiritual Life

C HRISTIAN LIFE, living in Christ by the Spirit, is a life in loving communion with God, others, and every living creature. The Trinitarian doctrine is expressive of what it means to participate in the life of God through Jesus Christ in the Spirit. A fresh understanding of God as Father, Son, and Spirit, and the understanding of person as a distinct one toward and for the other which is at the heart of the Trinitarian doctrine, can greatly enrich our understanding of Christian living. The Trinity is not a model for how to live the Christian life, however. Rather, understanding the grammar of the Trinity helps us to live freely in and from the gift given through the Word and in the Spirit, to speak the Trinitarian mystery with our whole lives.

The Christian spiritual life is not principally concerned with the solitary journey, with introspection, or with self-perfection. Christian spirituality does not refer to just one dimension of Christian living. Rather, Christian spirituality describes the whole of the Christian life, being conformed to the person of Christ, brought to fuller participation in com-

munion with God and others through the gift of the Holy
Spirit. Human persons are created for loving communion
with the Father, through Christ, in the Holy Spirit. God is
Love, the life that is pouring itself forth. God's very being is
the gift of Love, given and giving as gift.

What are the implications of a thoroughly Trinitarian
understanding of God for those dimensions of the Christian
life ordinarily associated with the spiritual life? From a revitalized understanding of the Trinity, how might we view holiness, vocation, asceticism, discernment, healing and wholeness, the Christian's engagement in society or "the world,"
prayer, contemplation and action, mysticism—in a word, the
various elements that make up the nomenclature of the
Christian spiritual life?

Because the Trinitarian doctrine expresses the profoundly
relational character of the divine mystery, an explicitly Trinitarian Christian spirituality is necessarily ecclesial and sacramental. By sharing in the mission of Christ and Spirit in a
community of discipleship which expresses and receives its
identity in its sacramental life, one grows in fuller communion
in the one Love. From the perspective of a Trinitarian spirituality, the various dimensions and disciplines of the spiritual
life spring from and draw us back to the celebration of
Christ's mysteries in word and sacrament within his Body ani-
mated by the Spirit.

A series of juxtapositions follows. In looking at various
elements of the spiritual life, we will compare and contrast a
revitalized Trinitarian approach with earlier, pre-conciliar approaches. It must be recognized that such a strategy runs the
risk of overstating differences, failing to give fair account of
highly intricate historical realities laden with delicate nuance.

Earlier approaches to the various dimensions of the Christian spiritual life were much more complex than they may appear in what follows. And what may appear to be a somewhat negative picture of the spiritual life in earlier epochs did, in fact, provide rich reserves of hope and promise for countless generations.

Holiness

The notion of the holy or holiness has its roots in an understanding of God as the Holy One. Holiness is something that is said of God, the One who is different from and other than human beings. Often this notion is accompanied by a sense of God as the absolutely other; that which is apart; that which is different; that which is in the order of the transcendent. By extension, the term "holy" applies to persons or objects, times, groups and peoples who are associated with the transcendent, those who are in relationship to God who is, above all, holy.

In Christian tradition the holy person has sometimes been seen as the one who, because of a higher calling, is separated from and placed above others for nobler purposes. He or she is set apart geographically or enclosed behind cloister walls, distanced from the everyday concerns of life in the world, removed from the ordinary pursuits of domestic and civic life.

The eremitical, monastic, and other contemplative ways of life are properly understood as ways of deification, entering into the mystery of the communion in one Love so as to show it forth. In Trinitarian perspective, even and especially the one who is called to a radically solitary life gives witness to this communion, for the God perceived and pursued in solitude is the three in one Love.

It may be helpful to recall that most Christian monastic traditions ("monastic," "monasticism," "monk" are rooted in *monos,* meaning "alone") give particular attention to the common life and the requirements of living together with others. The monastic way may be best understood as the solitary life pursued together with others, giving expression to the mystery of the divine communion in common prayer and common work.

If God is for us in the economy of salvation, then the holiness of God cannot be mirrored most perfectly in the one who is distant, aloof, and unaffected by the actual historical circumstances that affect the great number of human beings. If God is understood as Father, Son, Spirit toward us, for us, with us, and in us, then holiness will be understood to lie in setting aside, standing apart from or above self-absorption, moving beyond self-preoccupation, self-indulgence, self-fixation. Holiness rests in becoming persons conformed to the image of God in us, being toward and for another, for others, and for God. Being holy is being alive in the glory of God that transforms. The holy person is the one transfigured by living in the communion of Christ's Body in the Spirit. God's very nature is ecstatic and fruitful, outpouring, superabundant Love, manifest in Christ transfigured, in being toward the Father in self-giving Love. God's own holiness does not lie in being a self-subsistent self, but in self-donation, self-giving Love that is the very glory of God shining in the face of Jesus transfigured. The divine life, of its very nature, goes out, sends forth, in ecstatic and fecund love.

In this view, "holiness" or "holy" does not refer only to those who are called to live away from the ordinary demands of life in the world, set apart to pursue a specifically religious or spiritual vocation, free of those concerns that occupy the time and energy of the vast number of people in the church: child rearing and job security and taxpaying and planning for retirement. Rather, authentic Christian holiness is realized by living in communion as Christ's Body through the Spirit amidst the vicissitudes and interruptions of life in a highly complex and fragmented world. It is precisely here and now that God is glorified in our own *ecstasis*, our own ecstatic, outpouring life in love in response to God's loving *ecstasis* through Christ in the Spirit. In this view, self-preoccupation and self-absorption are major hurdles to holiness. We find the deepest gift of who we are and who we are called to be as Christ's Body in the Spirit, not in standing apart from the affairs of human life and its concerns, but by entering into personal communion with the God who is Father, Son, and Spirit. This we do precisely by embracing the human reality as Christ did in the power of the Spirit, living amidst the human reality in a way that gives glory to God by the self-gift which the Spirit alone makes possible. In self-giving, ecstatic love we enter into communion with all those with whom Christ lived and for whom Christ died as God's own Word of undying love and life.

Vocation

"Vocation" is an essential term in the nomenclature of the Christian spiritual life. In many currents of Christian spirituality, vocation has been understood to mean a particular form of life, namely, the vowed religious life or ordination to the priesthood. Both require abstinence from sexual relations, the foregoing of marriage and children. Religious life and priesthood were regarded as the true Christian vocations, the serious Christian life. They were often judged to be higher callings, nobler vocations, ways of life intrinsically superior to marriage and the single life.

The Second Vatican Council expressed helpful correctives to this view of vocation in three of its documents: the Dogmatic Constitution on the Church, *Lumen Gentium*; the Decree on the Renewal of Religious Life, *Perfectae Caritatis*; and the Decree on the Apostolate of the Laity, *Apostolicam Actuositatem*. All the various ways in which the baptized live in the communion of Christ's Body in the Spirit constitute authentic Christian vocations. Different people participate in different ways in the communion in one Love, thereby rendering the mystery concrete in a rich range of life forms. One's vocation is to be discerned within the concrete circumstances of one's life, in what one has been given by nature and grace, in living with and from an appreciation of one's life as a gift. Vocation, then, is a way of presencing Christ and the Spirit, rendering present the mystery of the three in one Love in a particular and irreplicable manner. Not a puzzle to be painstakingly figured out by searching for some abstract notion of God's will, discerning one's vocation occurs within the givenness of one's life as one seeks to answer the questions: Where do I fit in the rich and complex communion in the one Love? What is my part in the struggle against evil? What is my place in creating a counter-community to combat the reign of Satan? How can I live the one and only life I have as a gift through and through?

The Christian vocation is to receive the Word of God and keep it in the presence and power of the indwelling Spirit sending us forth to enlighten, enliven, guide, and heal. The Christian vocation is lived in various ways and walks of life. This diversity is properly understood in light of the universal call to holiness rooted in baptism, strengthened in confirmation, and renewed in frequent celebration of the Eucharist.

And so it is to be lamented that, even in our own day, the ordained ministry is still understood by many to set one apart from, and often above, the women and men one is ordained to serve. The ordained is viewed as possessing a special ontological character that empowers the priest alone to dispense grace and sacrament. But if the ordained ministry is a participation in the life of Christ the *servant*, and if all ministries—ordained and non-ordained—are rooted in the mission of Christ and Spirit manifest in the grand economy of salvation, then those who are ordained cannot properly be envisioned as set apart from or above others in holiness.

In the past, most expressions of religious life emphasized the vow of obedience as a means of becoming more closely conformed to Christ. In part, this entailed bringing one's dispositions and decisions into conformity with the will of God as expressed in the directives of the religious superior, often understood to voice the will of God for the community and its members. This, too, has been given considerable nuance in the teaching of the Second Vatican Council, particularly in the Decree on the Renewal of Religious Life, *Perfectae Cari-*

tatis, which draws attention to the need for shared discernment, decision making, and responsibility in religious life.

In our revitalized Trinitarian perspective, obedience (which in its etymology means "to listen to," or "to hear") requires attentiveness to the Word and to the Spirit active and present in a multiplicity of voices and events and in the lives of all those who live in communion as Christ's Body in the Spirit, all whose lives give prophetic utterance to the life-giving word of the gospel. Everyone baptized into Christ's Body is called to embrace a life of obedience to the Word and of submission to the Spirit's lead, not just those bound by vows to the religious life.

Asceticism

Christian asceticism refers to the discipline of various exercises by which one seeks to be conformed to Christ. Indeed, there can be no serious pursuit of the Christian spiritual life without such discipline. In the history of Christian spirituality, virginity and celibacy developed early on as forms of Christian asceticism, embodied signs of the anticipation of the *eschaton*, the future fulfillment in which Christ will be all in all. The virgin, and the one who embraced celibacy for the kingdom of God, was looked upon as a living sign of this anticipation, this waiting for the fulfillment and completion characteristic of all Christian living in the Spirit. But virginity and celibacy have too often been viewed as superior forms of Christian life. Celibacy came to be seen as a form of the solitary life precluding explicit sexual expression, marriage and, in some interpretations, any and all engagement in affective relationships. Sexual abstinence was often regarded as an essential component of the Christian spiritual life seriously pursued. Any survey of Christian history will show that the spirituality of the laity came to be seen as derivative and lesser, in part, because of the priority given to virginity and celibacy. Christian *ascesis* has all too often been understood narrowly as mortification of the flesh, and has not been applied consistently to other demanding aspects of the Christian life such as the rigorous sacrifices entailed in marital and family life, especially caring for one's children; the uncertainties of agrarian life; the daily struggles for mere subsistence; complex decisions about the use and disposition of goods; the chaste exercise of sexuality for non-celibates; responsibility for the earth; the discipline required for education and study; proper care and exercise of the body including nutrition, diet, balance of leisure and work; and the tedium of too much work. These dimensions of Christian life were rarely addressed in treatments of the rigors of asceticism. Yet this is the very "stuff" of Christian living—from font, to table, to cross. It is, however, important to recognize that in current Catholic teaching, greater attention has been given to the manifold dimensions of Christian life, and to the necessity of bringing them all to bear on the task of being conformed to Christ.

We give glory to God by being conformed to the person of Christ, brought into communion with God and one another in the Spirit. This is a communion of interpersonal love which calls for the discipline of cultivating, nurturing, and sustaining rightly ordered relationships of equality, interdependence, mutuality. The disciplines and exercises that enable us to create a world of communion and justice amidst the vicissitudes of life in this world constitute the asceticism appropriate to a thoroughgoing Trinitarian spirituality.

In an age such as ours when the spiritual life is sometimes understood as a path of self-realization and personal fulfillment, it is important to recognize that Christian life in the Spirit is both gift *and* task. As such, it calls for rigorous discipline and sharp discernment. Asceticism describes the disciplines by which we learn to relate to the body and to all created reality in a manner that is enlivened by the Spirit. Through sustained *ascesis* we gradually refine our attitudes to life and to the world so as to receive the gift of God's life. Christian asceticism is a way of consistently turning away from the allurements that divert our mind and heart from God's constant coming as gift, opening the self to receive the life and love that are God's own gift to us.

It is a facile reading of a complex history to suggest that earlier approaches to Christian asceticism denigrated the human body and devalued the material order as an obstacle to the pursuit of the nobler life of the spirit. Irish monks are often the proverbial whipping boys when such a case is being made. In early Christian centuries, Irish monks were drawn to the jagged mountains on the west coast of Ireland. Far removed from kin and townsfolk, they took shelter in stone huts overlooking a cold black sea, braced against the harsh, wet weather. There they lived lives of prayer and manual work, finding sustenance on the fish they took from the sea and the vegetation from the rocks.

On my thirty-third birthday I visited one of the most famous of these early monastic settlements, Skellig Michael.

Perched on two huge rocks that jut out of the dark sea off the coast of County Kerry in southwest Ireland are the remnants of the beehive-like huts built by the early monks. The long journey to Skellig Michael, or Saint Michael's Rock, is not an easy one. More often than not, the small motor boat which leaves port for Skellig Michael only once a day is unable to make the journey because of rough seas and pounding rain. The few travelers who made the journey on my one and only visit to Skellig Michael commented in various ways and different tones on the "dreadful" and "otherworldly lifestyle" of the monks. I, on the other hand, imagined these solitary figures clustered together in self- and mutual help as they sought to turn away from the many diversions of, yes, even early Irish agrarian life. I could envision them turning to God in constant prayer, so as to breathe in God along with that wild air whipping the blacker-than-coal rocks and filling the little lungs of the thousands and thousands of puffins perched on the cliffs of Skellig Michael. And, even and especially there, far off the southwestern coast of Ireland, learning how to receive the gift of God's life—in the sea, the air, the sky, even those puffins, but, above all, in the sharing of life and work and prayer in the pursuit of the one Love.

Discernment and Spiritual Direction

Discernment of spirits and spiritual direction have until rather recently been looked upon as necessary for vowed religious, monks and nuns, and the clergy, those living a serious spiritual life or the life of a "full-time" Christian "professional." It was sometimes thought that a greater burden lay on those who had taken on the "real" form of Christian life signified by religious vows or a promise of celibacy. Discernment of spirits and spiritual direction were practices quite rare among the laity, who were thought to be taken up with worldly affairs rather than with the nobler matters of the spiritual life.

In many earlier approaches, discernment and direction emphasized engaging in techniques for charting the action of the Spirit in an individual's life. This was done in consultation with a spiritual director or mentor, one judged to be wise in the ways of the Spirit. In practice, discernment of spirits was often relegated to a concentrated period of time during which one was engaged in specific exercises aimed at making a choice for Christ and embracing, or electing, a particular way of life or vocation, rather than being understood as an ongoing, lifelong process of attending to the various movements of the Spirit's presence, the interplay of light and darkness in one's own life and in the wider world. Regularly scheduled retreats were most often conducted in such a way as to feed the spiritual life of clergy or vowed religious women and men, without due attention to the spiritual needs of Christians in other walks of life in the world.

All of this stands in contrast to an understanding of discernment and direction as the gift and task of all who live in communion with Christ's Body in the Spirit. Beholding the glory of God and growing in communion require seeing the whole world and every activity within it as the locus of the Spirit's presence and action, engaging in the struggle against the forces of evil and darkness in the wider world as well as in our own lives.

Figuring out what it means to be a disciple of Christ in the world entails striving for a clear perception of the purpose of one's life and the shape of one's destiny, but always in view of God's providential plan for all humanity and the whole world. The dualisms between sacred and secular, between clergy and lay, between the professional and lay Christian are untenable if we live from a Trinitarian spirituality. All creation is the arena in which God is working out the providential plan of salvation. The presence of God is to be discerned and the direction of the Spirit discovered just as much in the ordinary, mundane, routine dimensions of life and work as in sacred times and spaces set aside for prayer and contemplation.

Discernment and direction are well thought of as disciplines whereby we stay awake, alert—indeed, vigilant—in the search for the divine presence in every dimension of daily living. Even while recognizing the need for skilled guidance in the life of the Spirit, we need not restrict these disciplines to the exercises undertaken during a specific time frame, while on retreat, under the guidance of a director. Living in and from a Trinitarian spirituality requires the lifelong discipline of cultivating a discerning heart able to recognize the direction of the Spirit in human life, history, the church, the world. This is a large mandate. Because most of us need help in following the Spirit's lead, we do well to profit from the various rules of discernment available to us, be they those offered in Paul's Letter to the Galatians, in John Cassian's *Conferences* and *Institutes*, or in Ignatius Loyola's *Spiritual Exercises*. Indeed, principles for discernment may be well thought of as a kind of grammar, the rules to which we look in seeking to fulfill the mandate to give expression to the mystery of the three in one Love in all our living.

Healing

Another aspect of growth in the Christian spiritual life is healing and wholeness. The Christian tradition has given a great deal of attention to the spiritual and corporal works of mercy. Concern for the healing of the body as well as of the soul is expressed in the church's sustained, continuing commitment to the care of the poor, the sick, the suffering, and the dying. This commitment has taken the form of the early church's care for the widow and the orphan, the response of communities of apostolic women religious to the pressing needs of their day, the ministry of educating poor immigrants and refugees, and the continuing struggle of women religious today to meet the needs of the sick and dying in the face of the diminishing numbers of sisters, severe economic constraints, and shifting values in the medical profession-become-health-care-industry.

The merits of the Christian tradition's commitment to healing and wholeness notwithstanding, it must be recognized that many previous approaches to healing and wholeness rested on a dualist anthropology, that is to say, an understanding of the human person as made up of opposing parts: body and soul, matter and spirit. Indeed, the very distinction between corporal and spiritual works of mercy bespeaks such a view of the human being: corporal—of or relating to the body; spiritual—of or relating to the spirit or the soul. It is unfortunate that in practice, if not in theory, spiritual works of mercy were seen as having greater value. The interest in pentecostalism and healing in the Roman Catholic Church in the post-conciliar period, to say nothing of similar eruptions at various points in the history of Christian spirituality, indicates that dualist understandings of human personhood are misleading and ultimately unsatisfactory in the quest for an integrated and holistic sense of Christian life.

Contemporary approaches to healing and wholeness informed by a Trinitarian spirituality consider the human person as a unity, a mystery of quite complex dimensions. In such a perspective, greater emphasis is given to the interrelationship among the various dimensions of the person within one's whole embodied personhood: one's relationship to the givenness of one's psyche, to one's gifts and limits, to the earthly reality of one's own body, to one's beloved, family, community, to the whole earth and to God. As we grow in appreciation of the interrelationship of the various dimensions of the self, we receive clues for understanding the importance of relating rightly to the various dimensions of life beyond the self. And, as we grow in rightly ordered relationship to others, to creation, and to God, we come to a fuller appreciation of the need to relate rightly to the other seemingly irreconcilable dimensions of our own selves.

Social Responsibility

Contemporary approaches to the Christian spiritual life recognize the Spirit's presence not just in one's own life, but in the wider social order, particularly in areas having to do with social justice. One of the most deleterious effects of focusing attention on a God divorced from the economy of salvation, or on a God who exists in the solitude of the solitary One, rather than on the creative, saving, sanctifying activity of Father, Son, and Spirit in the economy of salvation, has been a rather singular concentration on individual sanctification, often to the neglect of social and political concerns. In some earlier approaches to the spiritual life, concern for others meant being charitable to those in one's immediate family, neighborhood, workplace, and/or community and, by extension, being charitable to others in the world at large.

All too often, the term "ethics" was virtually synonymous with sexual ethics. Responsibility for the social, political, economic order, i.e., the ethics of social justice, was by and large not thought to be an essential part of Christian spiritual life and growth, though even an individualistic approach stressed justice as embodied in the eighth and tenth commandments and in the duties of one's station in life. The problem may have been with a narrow understanding of the meaning of justice. From the perspective of a contemporary Trinitarian spirituality, justice means rendering to each person according to his or her need, creating a world in which all may grow, establishing rightly ordered relationships in accord with the providential plan of God for humanity. Today there is a clearer recognition of the fact that creating communities of justice in service of the communion in one Love is not merely desirable, but required. Charity is without question a requirement for real growth and development in the spiritual life. Justice is no less a requirement.

A thoroughgoing Trinitarian spirituality entails the recognition that God's providential plan for the world involves absolutely every dimension of existence: every inch and ounce of creation is embraced by the loving God through Jesus Christ in the Spirit. A Trinitarian spirituality is at once personal and relational, inclusive of every human concern and commitment, giving particular attention to the last, littlest, and least of the earth, to those who are most wounded and weak in the church and in the world. It is inclusive even and especially of those who are often judged to be non-persons. It is also inclusive of all forms of non-human life and of all creation, indeed the whole world, which has received the gift given in the sending of God's Son and the life-giving Spirit dwelling in human hearts, breathing and gathering up all the living into the glory of God.

Prayer

Prayer and worship are central to the Christian spiritual life. Indeed, without a heart awakened in prayer and worship, there will be no possibility whatsoever of receiving the gift of God's love through Christ in the Spirit. It is true that prayer is a discipline, a practice. But prayer, the silent, loving, attentive heart at rest in God, is a whole way of life. Prayer is living from the heart in response to the life which pours itself forth: Love. Quite simply, prayer is seeking to be in communion with the Father, through the Son, in the Spirit. All forms of prayer—petition, adoration, thanksgiving, lament, doxology, quiet recollection and repose, listening long and lovingly to the beating of the heart of God—are ways of participation in the mission of Word and Spirit. Prayer is nothing more or less than breathing with the Spirit, speaking the

Word. This is as true of communal, liturgical prayer as it is of individual, personal prayer. Participation in the divine life, and the manner of living to which this participation gives rise, as well as the various disciplines and practices for growing in the Christian spiritual life, all spring from a heart which is awake, vigilant, in prayer. It is in and through prayer that we are seized and saturated by Love's giving.

Understandings of Christian prayer have been profoundly influenced by the historical and theological development of the doctrine of the Trinity. The view of prayer as communication in the manner of a one-to-one conversation has occupied a central place in many approaches to the practice of prayer in the Christian tradition. Those Christian churches shaped by strong sacramental and liturgical traditions ordinarily keep the communitarian nature of all Christian prayer to the fore. But, even within the context of Christian worship, prayer is often understood as an essentially private, individual exercise. It is likened to a conversation between the individual human person and God, conceived of as a divine individual. Spiritual exercises and strategies of spiritual direction have often been shaped in terms of such a one-to-one model. This remains true even in our own day. Prayer is usually associated with the journey inward; figuring out God's will for oneself; discovering what it means to be a disciple of Christ; invoking God's blessing for oneself and those one holds dear; and examining one's failures and making amends for what one has done or not done. Such an approach to prayer and spiritual direction can reflect an understanding of God who is the other partner in a personal dia-

logue and who discloses hidden purposes and plans in the se-
cret of the individual's heart.

An approach to prayer altogether Trinitarian, on the
other hand, emphasizes the communal, relational, indeed,
the social character of all prayer. The deepest kind of prayer
is a communion in the Spirit enlivening Christ's Body, a way
of living from the gift of God's love in the human heart urg-
ing us to be and to build the Body of Christ in the church
and in the world. Prayer is relationship with and contemplation of God at the heart of human life, history, the church,
the world, much more than it is a repertoire of pious devo-
tions or meditation techniques. These latter are properly understood as means to the end: beholding the glory of God in
any expression and in all forms of authentic communion.

In such perspective, prayer is not yet another activity relegated to specific times and places in which the individual
talks to the solitary One of heavenly solitude. Prayer disposes
and enables us to participate in the contemplative dimension
of everyday living, recognizing the presence and action of the
Holy Spirit with us at every turn. All authentic Christian living is properly understood as doxological. That is to say,
Christian life itself, when it is an expression of our long and
loving desire for God, is an act of prayer and praise and
glory. This is true of the whole of life—not just this or that
part or piece of it. Every dimension of life in Christ is taken
up into the ongoing economy of salvation through a life of
prayer. Prayer, then, while it may be viewed as conversation
and communication in dialogue is, in Trinitarian perspective,
more properly understood as ongoing participation in the

communion of persons, divine and human, which comprises God's providential plan for all humanity. Indeed, above all else, prayer is that which enables the Christian people to see the ordinary and the everyday earthly reality as the very arena of God's presence and action, the place where we are invited to live in and from the presence of God through communion in the Spirit which makes of us Christ's Body.

There is always a risk in giving advice in the ways of prayer. Indeed there is wisdom in the truth that the deepest kind of prayer cannot be taught. But over many years I have come to two insights about prayer which may be of help to others. First, it does not matter so much *when* I pray. But it does matter *that* I pray. The second insight, which has made all the difference, is this: I have a hard time praying—except for all the time. What this means quite simply is that when I engage in regular, disciplined prayer, be it *lectio divina*, quiet recollection, or participation in liturgical worship or in the recitation of the psalms alongside others in a community, it is very often a struggle. Not always, but often. But, then, when I simply attend to my breathing, catch a view of a hummingbird feeding at my window, allow myself to be gripped by the ache expressed in the grimace of a postal worker, hear the language of loss and hope regained in the simple narrative of someone still struggling with terminal illness, see words wonderfully strung together on a page to evoke in me a sense now of tenderness and then of tragedy, it is then—almost all the time—that I know myself to be drawn into that holy communion in one Love. And there I am held in the knowledge that all that I am and all that I have is first and finally gift. Prayer is a way of living with, in, and from that gift. All the time.

Contemplation and Action

Not only does a revitalized understanding of the Trinity cast new light on the nature of Christian prayer, it also helps us to understand the age-old tension between prayer and action, or contemplation and action. Prayer describes the movement of the human heart toward ever fuller participation in the life of God. Prayer is the response of one's whole person—the whole of oneself—to God's initiative as this is experienced in one's own life, in the life of one's people, and in the creative, saving, sanctifying activity of God, Father, Son, Spirit, in the grand economy of salvation.

To speak of prayer as the movement of the human heart, as the language of longing and desire, is not to confine the heart to the region of private, individual feelings or emotions in opposition to other dimensions of the person. The heart describes the deepest, most fundamental center of the person, the core of the human being. As such, the image of the heart is used in the Hebrew (*leb*, *lebab*) and Christian scriptures (*kardia*), as well as in the history of Christian spirituality, to describe the whole person. A person doesn't *have* a heart but *is* the heart. "Heart" is the name for *affectus*, affectivity, or the affective dimension of the person. "Affectivity" here means the very openness of the human being to be touched by another, by others, and by God. *Affectus*, "affectivity," or "heart" names the human capacity to be toward and for the other, for others, for God. As such, the heart is not a region of private and personal feelings to the exclusion of other dimensions of human life but, rather, is inclusive of communal and social realities. To have a heart is to possess the capacity to be in relation. The heart describes the human being's openness to relate to the real, to the "out-there," to that which is other as distinct from the self. It is the very being within human beings toward the good, the longing in each of us for light, for life, for love. And it is that in us which wants to give and to be life, light, and love for others.

If prayer is the movement of the heart, the language of longing and desire for interpersonal communion with God and others, then it is not well thought of principally as a private exercise or an isolated activity. All disciplines and activities of prayer have as their end the glory of God, the God who is best glorified by the relations of interpersonal love, by interpersonal communion, by our participation in the self-giving love of Father, Son, and Spirit.

Prayer as the response of the whole person to the divine initiative, which is disclosed not just in the recesses of one's interior life but in the whole economy of salvation, cannot be construed in such a way that it exists in opposition to action. Prayer is the "speechifying" of desire, the expressivity of the heart's desire. That is to say, prayer is the effort of the human heart to be, precisely by being in relation. The openness to relation that is the constitutive dimension of human beings is itself an absence, a longing for completion and fullness in and through the other, with others, in God.

Human personhood is both gift and task. We are recipients of the one and only life we have. We become the persons we are called to be by living freely and acting responsibly with and from the gift we have received. Prayer of the heart is expressed in simple, loving attention to the gift of

God's presence and action—in human life, history, the church, the world—as well as through those activities by which we seek to participate more fully in establishing an authentic communion of persons related in equality, interdependence, and mutuality. Contemplation, the non-pragmatic gaze of love upon Love's gift, and the action of establishing, nurturing, sustaining relations of interpersonal communion and justice, especially for the last, littlest, and least among us, are ineluctably related movements of the one desire impelling the single human heart toward God.

From a Trinitarian perspective, prayer may be thought of as a methodical, organized, discursive meditation on the mystery of God's love. Prayer's exercise may indeed give rise to quiet contemplation, the mind's undisturbed gaze upon or, better, *toward* or *in* the unfathomable mystery of Love. Or it may take the form of simple repose in the life and love of God. But prayer finds its fullest expression when the attentive human heart participates in the very life of God, responding to the manifold ways in which God comes in Christ through the presence and power of the Spirit. Prayer is response to gift: in attentiveness, in wonder, in delight, in adoration, in thanksgiving, in humble petition, in reflective study, in ready listening. And in tending to the needs of the sick, in feeding, in washing and in waiting, in building bridges between families, communities, peoples, and nations. It is not at all helpful, then, to think of prayer as springing from or nourishing one's spiritual life as if such a life existed in a separate compartment of our selves.

Such a view of prayer may aid us in overcoming the unhelpful separations between spiritual life and secular life, sa-

cred and profane, church and world, gospel and culture. The
Trinity names the mystery of three in one Love: the God
who is Father, Son, and Spirit in human life, history, the
church, and the world *is* the very God who is God. So human
persons are, and are called to be ever more, unified, integrated, whole. This wholeness, indeed holiness, rests in the
deepest core of one's being, in the heart.

There is in each of us a single heart called to respond to
the one God made manifest through Christ in the Spirit
present and active in human life, history, church, and world.
A Trinitarian-based approach thus serves to correct skewed
notions of the relationship between action and contemplation. Informed by the doctrine of the Trinity, prayer and action are not relegated to separate spheres: the sacred and the
secular, church and world, the spiritual life and the domain of
the secular and profane. There is one God who, known and
loved in the creative, saving, and sanctifying activity of the
Father, Son, and Spirit, is toward us and for us and for the
whole world.

Mysticism

Often understood as the fullest expression of Christian
life and prayer, mysticism is usually spoken of in terms of an
immediate, that is unmediated, experience of the divine mystery. The individual soul encounters and is gradually, pro-
gressively, drawn into the deepest recesses of divine life.
From this perspective, the goal of the mystical journey is
complete union with God. The mystic is usually thought to
be a solitary, often eccentric figure, someone quite unlike the
ordinary Christian. Most approaches to mystical experience

in the Christian tradition, past and present, hold that mysticism—mystical experience, the mystical life—is extraordinary. Mystical experience is not the ordinary outcome of the baptismal call to the life of holiness and the pursuit of virtue; for this reason it has often been suspect, even in the Christian tradition. The mystical life has been thought to be highly unusual, made possible by special graces. But the very notion of an unusual experience of God can undercut the priority of ordinary, earthly reality, of human life in its grandeur and vulnerability as the very locus where God is known and loved, indeed experienced, through the creative, saving, sanctifying acts of Father, Son, and Spirit. The mystery to be experienced is the providential plan of God for human beings and the whole world, mediated in and through the Incarnate Word and in the specific, particular, earthy work of the Holy Spirit who brings about the reordering of all creation.

At the same time, it must be recognized that there are indeed ordinary and extraordinary forms of mysticism. There is continuity between them, yet experientially they may be quite different. Ordinary mysticism has just as much power and theological validity as extraordinary mysticism, yet extraordinary mysticism is also a charism that God gives for the uplifting of the church.

An approach to mysticism rooted in the Trinitarian mystery requires attention to the whole range of human experience in history, in the world, in culture, in human persons, and in the church wherein God's presence and action are discerned. The experience of union with God is to be found in every form of communion: affective, sexual, familial, artistic. It is to be found in the intellectual pursuit of truth, in the pursuit and apprehension of the good, and in the simple act of appreciating the beautiful. Every form of authentic communion is a potential avenue for union with God known in the sending of the Son and in the gift of the Spirit who enlightens, enlivens, guides, heals, and sends us forth to live in and from the mystery of God's love.

Is all Christian mysticism Trinitarian? While the writings of some mystics describe an experience of God as three in one Love, the writings of others seem to express little explicit Trinitarian consciousness. That is, there appears to be very little awareness of the communion of Father, Son, and Spirit as that reality which lies at the heart of Christian faith and life, and therefore of that mystery formative of all Christian religious experience as such, and all mystical experience precisely as Christian.

Why do some mystical writings seem to rely so little on explicit Trinitarian symbolism? It is conceivable that mystics perceive the basic truth that the grammar of the Trinitarian doctrine seeks to articulate, but when they try to express what they have perceived, words fall short. Or, it may be that the prevailing Christian doctrine of God had by a certain historical point so marginalized the Trinitarian mystery because of its esoteric and speculative character that Christian mystics of that time gravitated toward understandings of God with far less emphasis on the three in one Love.

Whatever the reason, it must be affirmed that Christian mysticism is a path through the economy of redemption in which God is revealed through Jesus Christ in the Holy Spirit. Thus it is to be expected that ordinarily Christian mystical experience, an experiential participation in the mystery of God, must in some way or another reflect the particularities of symbols, stories, and events central to Christian faith and life.

Light is at the core of the experience of the central Christian mystery: the Father's love seen in the Son through the presence of the Spirit. It is a piercing, shattering Light amidst the most agonizing, deadening darkness of absence. But absence is the place, the space for the Light's coming. Constantly. In the darkness, I see: all is iconic of the divine, shimmering in the Light that transfigures. Everything is related to everything else, created in the image of a God who exists in the relations of interpersonal love. This mystery we name "Father, Son, Spirit." And then we fall silent in wonder at the inadequacy of words, of names which cannot name the One whose name is beyond, and beneath, all naming, but who is known in the Word's *kenosis* and in the outpouring and bonding of the Spirit.

The various disciplines of the Christian spiritual life are simply the means by which we seek to participate, more contemplatively, in the mystery of three in one Love. The various terms that have formed the nomenclature of spiritual life—holiness, vocation, asceticism, discernment, healing and wholeness, social responsibility, prayer, contemplation and action, mysticism—all bespeak the truth that learning to receive is a lifelong process, never an entirely accomplished fact. The Christian spiritual life entails the ongoing, rigorous discipline of receptivity, of cultivating, nurturing, and sustaining a grateful heart for what is. All is gift, ours to receive, even that which awaits us at the end of the one and only life we have to live—which is given as gift.

CHAPTER SIX

In Prayerful Communion

T HE MYSTERY OF THE THREE IN ONE LOVE has been made manifest so that we might participate in the divine life. The words on these pages are intended to invite a deeper participation in the very life of the God who is Love, the One who is Giver, Given, and Gift/ing. As we come to know the love of the Father through the Son in the Spirit, we are able to recognize the magnitude of God's love in human life and creation, in the events of history, in our own lives and the lives of others, in the church, and in the wider world. But beholding the God who is Love, the One whose life is altogether gift, calls for cultivating, nurturing, and sustaining a heart attentive to Love in all its expressions, in its myriad manifestations.

What follows are fifteen points for prayerful reflection. This chapter is not to be read like the other chapters of this book. Rather, each point for reflection is to be considered slowly, carefully. In the spirit of *lectio divina*, sacred reading, select one point for prayer. Read it aloud. Chew over the syllables, each word, every phrase. Let the words sink into your deepmost heart. If your mind wanders, let it be. Gently come back, again and again, to the few words you have selected for prayer. Say the words aloud. Slowly. One by one. Again and again.

The heart is at peace, the mind is soothed in Light as we rest in the mystery of the three in one Love spoken in the few words of each point of reflection. An insight from an earlier chapter may come to mind to nourish the heart. Go back to it. Stay with it. Linger. Ponder the mystery of God's love long and lovingly. Listen long and lovingly to the beating of the heart of God who is Giver, Given, Gift/ing. Here and now.

Stay with just one point of reflection. Do not rush through. Where will you be when you get to where you think you are going? Nowhere at all, if not in communion with the three in one Love.

The words of the reflection may not speak at once; they may not nourish the heart at first glance. But be patient enough to stay with the words. Or with just one word.

Go back over and over again. These words may spark an image or call up a word from the scriptures. Go there. Stay with it: the word of God in scripture. You may be drawn to an image of the Trinity. Let your eyes rest on it. A song may stir in your heart. If so, then sing. With your lips, with your heart, with the whole of your life. Let your life be an endless hymn to Love's Pure Source, to Love Expressed, to Love Bonding. Embrace the words with the eye of the heart. And then be embraced by them.

Embraced by the words in prayerful reflection, you may then hear the Word beneath and beyond all the words: Love is speaking and breathing. Now.

TRINITARIAN SPIRITUALITY is a baptismal spirituality, a whole way of life through which we are conformed to Christ, anointed in the Spirit, and gifted by the Father.

ALL CHRISTIAN SPIRITUALITY is Trinitarian—a way of perceiving and being by which we are conformed to the person of Christ, brought into communion with God, other persons, and every living creature by the creative and bonding presence of the Holy Spirit, Love's Gift/ing.

A CHRISTIAN SPIRITUALITY *which is Trinitarian through and through is not concerned with just one dimension of life, such as prayer or the pursuit of holiness. Rather, the Christian spiritual life is the Christian life—living through Christ in the Spirit to the glory of God the Father.*

*W*E EXPERIENCE OURSELVES *most completely as recipients of God's self-giving. From this basic awareness of ourselves as recipients of gift, we come to recognize God as the Giver of all gifts, giving continually to the world in love: Father as originating Lover; Son as the perfect expression of that Love; Spirit as the unbounded activity of this Love.*

To LIVE A TRINITARIAN SPIRITUALITY is to be seized and saturated by the gift of Love. Our vocation is to live with, in, and from this gift—as stewards of all creation, guests in God's household. We become continuing expressions of the gift as we live from it, knowing ourselves to be in constant relation to its source.

We LEARN SOMETHING ABOUT GOD in the stories of the scriptures and in the symbols, images, and narratives of the Christian tradition. It is through the creative, saving, sanctifying action of Father, Son, and Spirit in human life, history, the church, and the world that we dare to speak the divine name above all naming: Love.

GOD'S LOVE IS MADE VISIBLE, *tangible, audible, in the self-emptying of God in Christ—in the Incarnation and on the cross. It is in and through this* kenosis *that God's presence is made manifest in the midst of the human reality, even and especially in our brokenness and vulnerability.*

GOD'S PRESENCE WITH AND FOR US *is immutably and irrevocably bestowed in the cross of Christ through which Love's gift is given unto death and into hell, assuring us that the Life who is Love cannot be extinguished, and that the power of Love prevails over all evil.*

THE DIVINE PRESENCE in the midst of human life, history, and all creation is recognized and celebrated in the sacramental life of the church, especially in the waters of baptism and at the table of the Eucharist. The Christian spiritual life consists of the movement from the font of baptism to the table of the Eucharist to the cross of our own suffering, diminishment, dying, and death. Our destiny as a Christian people is to live human life in all its dimensions in the presence of the divine.

WE ARE NOT SELF-MADE SELVES; our identity is not determined solely by others. Human life is Theonomous—*we are from God, toward God, for God. Each human person is destined for transformation by the glory of God, as seen in the Transfiguration of Christ, the foreshadowing of Love Given on the cross and Love Bonding with its Source in the Resurrection.*

THE FULLNESS OF HUMAN LIFE AND DESTINY lies in self-giving as a response to the gift of Love which is the self-gift of the Father, through the Son, in the Spirit. Through the gift which has been first given, we participate in the mission of Word and Spirit, cultivating, nurturing, and sustaining a world transformed in and by Love.

PRAYER AND OTHER DISCIPLINES of the Christian spiritual life have as their purpose God's greater glory, which is realized all the more as we are brought, in and through such spiritual disciplines, into fuller communion with the living God who is Love, named "Father, Son, Spirit."

PRACTICES OF THE SPIRITUAL LIFE help us to realize our destiny as receivers of God's gift, and to live freely from that gift. Thus, at the heart of the Christian spiritual life is the spiritual practice of receptivity, a rigorous discipline through which we learn how to receive and celebrate the gift of God's giving.

LIVING FREELY FROM THE GIFT requires that we embrace our destiny to offer ourselves as a gift through life and through death, seeing in human diminishment, weakness, and vulnerability—even and especially our own—the gift of God's constant coming.

A SPIRITUALITY WHICH IS ALTOGETHER TRINITARIAN enables us to see that we participate even now in the mystery of self-giving Love at the heart of the divine life. We do this all the more as we seek to live:

— *in childlike trust of the Father, confident in the utter reliability of God's fidelity and care for us.*

— *as Christ's Body, immersed with him in human life, history, the church, and the world, speaking a prophetic word of truth in love, tending to the needs of the last and littlest and least, giving the gift of self together with him unto death.*

— *sent by the Spirit dwelling in our deepmost hearts, the very life and love of God in us, to enlighten, enliven, guide, and heal a world both wondrous and wounded and a church still struggling and stumbling as it seeks to speak the language of mercy.*

In the end, words must give way to silence, creating a space for self-transcendence and communion. The words on these pages are meant to invite interpersonal communion with others, with every living creature, and with the living God named "Father, Son, Spirit." The words now give way to silence. As words are left behind and pages set aside, we enter the space which they create. This wide-open space is the region of wound and wisdom named "heart." It is in this place, which is not a place at all, where we live in prayerful communion with the living God. Seized by Love's pure light and saturated by Love's outpouring, the eye of the heart beholds the glory of God, three in the one Love, Giver, Given, Gift/ing: Love speaking and breathing. Receive the gift.

For Further Reading

Boff, Leonardo. *Trinity and Society*. Maryknoll, N.Y.: Orbis Books, 1988.

Coffey, David. Deus Trinitas: *The Doctrine of the Triune God*. New York: Oxford University Press, 1999.

Congar, Yves. *I Believe in the Holy Spirit*. New York: The Cross-road Publishing Co., 1997.

Cunningham, David S. *These Three Are One: The Practice of Trinitarian Theology*. Malden, Mass.: Blackwell Publishers, Inc., 1998.

Fatula, Mary Ann. *The Triune God of Christian Faith*. Collegeville, Minn.: The Liturgical Press, 1990.

Finn, Thomas M. *Early Christian Baptism and the Catechumenate: West and East Syria*. Collegeville, Minn.: The Liturgical Press, 1992.

———. *Early Christian Baptism and the Catechumenate: Italy, North Africa, and Egypt*. Collegeville, Minn.: The Liturgical Press, 1992.

Fortman, Edmund J. *The Triune God: A Historical Study of the Doctrine of the Trinity*. Eugene, Ore.: Wipf and Stock Publishers, 1999.

Gunton, Colin E. *The Promise of Trinitarian Theology*. Edinburgh, Scotland: T&T Clark, 1991.

Hill, William J. *The Three-Personed God: The Trinity as a Mystery of Salvation*. Washington, D.C.: The Catholic University of America Press, 1982.

Hunt, Anne. *What Are They Saying about the Trinity?* New York/ Mahwah, N.J.: Paulist Press, 1998.

———. *The Trinity and the Paschal Mystery: A Development in Recent Catholic Theology*. Collegeville, Minn.: The Liturgical Press, 1997.

Johnson, Elizabeth A. *She Who Is: The Mystery of God in Feminist Theological Discourse*. New York: The Crossroad Publishing Co., 1992.

Kasper, Walter. *The God of Jesus Christ*. New York: The Crossroad Publishing Co., 1989.

Kelly, Anthony. *The Trinity of Love: A Theology of the Christian God*. Collegeville, Minn.: The Liturgical Press/Michael Glazier, 1989.

LaCugna, Catherine Mowry. *God for Us: The Trinity and Christian Life*. San Francisco: Harper Collins, 1991.

———. "God in Communion with Us: The Trinity." In *Freeing Theology: The Essentials of Theology in Feminist Perspective*, edited by C. M. LaCugna, 83-114. San Francisco: Harper Collins, 1993.

LaCugna, Catherine Mowry, and Michael Downey. "Trinitarian Spirituality." In *The New Dictionary of Catholic Spirituality*, edited by Michael Downey, 968-82. Collegeville, Minn.: The Liturgical Press, 1993.

LaCugna, Catherine Mowry, and Kilian McDonnell. "Returning from 'The Far Country': Theses for a Contemporary Trinitarian Theology." *The Scottish Journal of Theology* 41 (1988): 191-215.

Marsh, Thomas. *The Triune God: A Biblical, Historical, and Theological Study*. Mystic, Conn.: Twenty-Third Publications, 1994.

McDonnell, Kilian. *The Baptism of Jesus in the Jordan: The Trinitarian and Cosmic Order of Salvation*. Collegeville, Minn.: The Liturgical Press, 1996.

Moltmann, Jürgen. *The Trinity and the Kingdom: The Doctrine of God*. San Francisco: Harper & Row, 1981.

O'Collins, Gerald. *The Tripersonal God: Understanding and Interpreting the Trinity*. New York/Mahwah, N.J.: Paulist Press, 1999.

Prokes, Mary Timothy. *Mutuality: The Human Image of Trinitarian Love*. New York/Mahwah, N.J.: Paulist Press, 1993.

Rahner, Karl. *The Trinity*. New York: The Crossroad Publishing Co., 1997.

Rusch, William G. *The Trinitarian Controversy*. Philadelphia: Fortress Press, 1980.

Zizioulas, John D. *Being as Communion: Studies in Personhood and the Church*. Crestwood, N.Y.: Saint Vladimir's Seminary Press, 1985.

Also by
Michael Downey

Hope Begins Where Hope Begins
ISBN 1-57075-185-4

A Main Selection of the Spiritual Book Associates

"In our chaotic world, we need people who cry
out with hope. That is what Michael Downey
does in a gentle way through telling stories, stories that touch the heart, stories that we can iden-
tify with. In these stories we find the presence of
our God of hope."

—*Jean Vanier*

"Downey gives such hope as encouragement, as
intruding gift, as bracing faith, and as lament. His
words are a persistent demand to be faithful witnesses to the hope to be found everywhere."

—*Megan McKenna*

Please support your local bookstore, or call 1-800-258-5838.

For a free catalogue, please write us at
Orbis Books, Box 308
Maryknoll NY 10545-0308
or visit our website at *www.maryknoll.org/orbis*

Thank you for reading *Altogether Gift.*
We hope you enjoyed it.